Duncan Minshull is a freelance audio producer and anthologist. He has previously published two books on walking, *While Wandering* (Random House) and *The Burning Leg* (Hesperus Press), and written about the subject for a variety of newspapers and magazines including *The Times*, *Financial Times*, the *Daily Telegraph*, *Slightly Foxed*, *Condé Nast Traveller*, *Psychologies* and *The Lady*. He lives in West London.

BENEATH MY FEET

Writers on Walking

–

Introduced and edited by
Duncan Minshull

 Notting Hill Editions

Published in 2018
by Notting Hill Editions Ltd
Mirefoot, Burneside, Kendal, Cumbria LA8 9AB
This edition published 2019

Cover design and artwork by Silvina De Vita
Artwork of walking figure on cover is based on an original drawing
by Ben Hollands, 2018
Illustration of shoes on page 168 by Ben Hollands, 2018
Typeset by CB Editions, London

Printed and bound in UK by Short Run Press

A CIP record for this book is available from the British Library

ISBN 978-1-912559-19-0

www.nottinghilleditions.com

To walk – This is a remarkable word. It comes from the Anglo-Saxon *wealcan* (to roll); whence *wealcere*, a fuller of cloth.

In Percy's *Reliques* we read:

> She cursed the weaver and the walker,
>
> The cloth that they had wrought.

To walk, therefore, is to roll along, as the machine, in felting hats or fulling cloth.

> – E. Cobham Brewer, *The Dictionary of Phrase and Fable,* 1894

Everyone should walk.

> – Werner Herzog, *Of Walking In Ice*, 1978

Contents

Duncan Minshull

– Introduction –

Hello. Just back from your daily walk? Was it down a lonely lane in sunlight or through a crowded city in drizzle? And apart from some air and exercise, why did you go? What set you off? Well – and here this editor's hopes gather apace – you'll turn the pages ahead for insights from a group of fellow travellers who have examined the need to put one foot in front of the other.

Walking takes the writer, the classic desk-dweller, out into the world – to meet with others, explore things, observe closely. Forward motion might affect him or her on the inside too – thoughts are stirred, which leads to creativity, to a verse or a paragraph possibly. Poets pace a rhythm for the lines to come. Novelists send characters across the pages. How many times has something happened to a hero and heroine after they snubbed their horse or car and walked to a place instead?

But perhaps a walk is best revealed by non-fiction accounts. In your hand is a selection of these, spanning the centuries, arranged loosely by theme. It features Petrarch in the 1330s, various golden ages of pedestrianism – Romantic, Victorian and Edwardian – and nods to the present day, with its own train of wanderers. All told, thirty-six of them will head over open fields, wild places, parks and gardens, and cities.

The essay form perfectly captures the trajectory of a walk, whilst extracts from journals, diaries and letters reflect all the impulses – the whys, hows and wherefores of footing it. By the time we next depart – or, as Henry David Thoreau puts it, 'silently unlatch the door' – there will be even more reasons to mull over. Incidentally, Thoreau advises us to stay out for four hours each time. Really? Does the duration of a walk matter? Let's not be distracted by that. Instead let's join some of those who've committed their footsteps to print.

Walking brings that air and exercise. It also lifts the spirits. Philosopher Søren Kierkegaard urged his niece Jette to be off, otherwise she'd lounge on a chaise longue all day. His letter to her of 1841 bursts with the joys of motion: 'health resides' this way. You can 'walk away from all morbid objections', reaching a state of 'bliss' that you bring home 'as safely as possible'. Surely it worked for her? Nicholas Shakespeare urges his own family to do likewise – two sleepy sons. At dawn on the fabulous Great Oyster Bay, all senses are sharpened before 'calm' comes to a father who leads them. And Rebecca Solnit is amongst 'purple lupine' and 'black butterflies', but as vital as the physical world ahead are the ideas forming in her head. She drifts satisfyingly from 'plans' to 'recollections'. She says she goes walking to think about walking.

Spirits truly soar when our walks take us into nature. Into extreme nature looming large – larger than Great Oyster Bay – where we might stutter and stumble against its sublime power. These places make us 'Lilliputian' according to the critic William Hazlitt, Alps-bound. Four travellers are abroad in such circumstances and we on our own lesser treks should admire them. The environmentalist John Muir (and dog) are flattened by the anvil heat of the Great Central Valley of California, only it's a small ordeal if a rare pine or chaparral is discovered. Victorian explorer Mary Kingsley flees a waterspout during her solo trek of the Cameroons, where she was asked by a local – where's your husband? Attuned to the woodlands of Maine is Henry David Thoreau, whose wade through snow and profound coldness demands of him a 'Puritan toughness'. Still, all suggestions of obsession and moral rectitude are in contrast with Mark Twain's clamber up the Rigi Kulm. Countless comic struggles lie in store for this Lilliputian, and nature will deal him a final, sly blow concerning sunrises. Fair to say, naive, gadabout Americans shouldn't fall for the allure of the Old World.

En route, appearances matter. Twain describes himself 'panoplied' in 'mountain costume'. There are no photographs, so assume tweeds and hobnail boots are de rigueur for 1880, just as Canada Goose and Timberlands cut it today. Gear is only partly about keeping warm and dry. Watch Chevalier de la Tocnaye saunter through Ireland in 1796 with 'fine shirts, three cravats, silk stockings, a powder bag', which seems to announce 'C'est Moi'. Whilst John Hillaby crosses deserts in the 1960s sporting shorts and tennis shoes, which whisper something else, something akin to: They Do The Job. For some it matters how an identity is projected, and this is true of city life where the streets are runways for dandies, flaneurs, anyone modish or transgressive. Novelist George Sand took to Paris in gent's attire – coat, suit, iron-heeled boots – making her 'fearless' and free to explore everywhere. Less as a woman wanting to be seen as a man, more as a figure wanting to be ignored, jostled, passed by; one of a 'desert of men' going about their daily business on the boulevards.

Before the city streets are trod, however, there's a view on reaching them, with the naturalist Richard Jefferies. Accompanying him down a country lane is immersive: exquisite eye-views of flowers and tiny insects, smells of sweet scents, and meetings with locals so genial and unhurried. Walk into wellbeing (as Kierkegaard says to Jette) and we are ready for anything. Later, as the sun dips, a different 'process of mind' is required when a local station for London nears. At the other end of the track we join a metropolitan flow, grasses still stuck to jackets, yet accepting that most paths, wherever they go, bring us back to the bricks and the bustle, the exhilaration and the anxiety: Jefferies noted this course of moods in 1883, and his bitter-sweetness speaks for now, after our own day in the country draws to a close.

What is the phrase? 'Walk fast in the country and stroll about in towns.' True or not, it implies there are different words for moving through the country and negotiating urban areas. Our fellow travellers have been in fields, on shores, up mountains. They have been ambling, rambling, tramping, trekking, stomping and striding. They have also skipped and leapt and swung to destinations. Such words suggest regular, uninterrupted strides with few obstacles met or doubts in the mind. Cities, however, are more compromised places, with their distractions and dead ends, their populations all present and pressing. Words for pounding the pavement are different – for a different experience beneath the feet.

Some take short, edgy strolls. Edward Hoagland does the rounds of his neighbourhood (he 'gobbles' the blocks), which enables him to witness a variety of types spilling outdoors in warm weather. Sure, there are buildings to look at, exotic aromas rising from sundry nooks, but it's the people with their behavioural tics and snatches of speech implying 'energy' and 'misery' – this is what he loves close up.

Christopher Hope, on the other hand, is unable to cross the road – too much traffic, except it's a thrill taking the plunge 'with elbows high' and relying on visibility to reach the other side. Then, as the light fades, a familiar unease: should we even be walking some streets? For Kamila Shamsie it is to do with which city she's in and occasionally her 'trepidation' is more present than any real and ready danger.

Someone else is in the gloaming: Virginia Woolf seeking a shop that will sell her a pencil, even if this is an 'excuse' to wander far and savour changes at street level under growing lamplight. The trick is to 'pass', 'dally', 'stop' as the mind wanders too, reacting to shifts of colour, altered states of offices and houses, and sightings of residents at illuminated windows. What do these lives hold? A simple shopping trip becomes expansive and complicated, and Woolf realises 'we are no longer ourselves' once the dusk thickens to darkness. She moves further into it.

Will Self embraces the transforming effect of night, abetted on a journey not by lamplight but by modern neon. It's three miles from restaurant to hotel, almost like a hike in the country, and 'traverse' is the word he uses. Fitfully-lit gloom throws up striking visuals, presents an idea he calls 'reverse paranoia' – Your views on that, dear reader? – and offers one more law of pedestrianism: that moving forward can take us back. The rhythm of walking lifts the spirits, spurs creativity *and* releases memories. Self's nightwalk reminds him of earlier times. London Bridge wafts by, as do scenes from New York and Varanasi, each with their own sights and sounds and encounters. He has visited three other places whilst traversing doggedly towards his bed.

Returning to the daylight hours, it's worth catching up with William Hazlitt – albeit briefly, because he's opinionated and can't stop himself. He's opinionated on an interesting point, though – should we go it alone or with others? You'd think he'd be in the latter camp, given his desire to be heard by all. No: he considers it impossible to think and talk to a friend at the same time, and besides any friend will get in the way, probably ruin the sights. Only if the sights are grand (pyramids and deserts) and remind us of our Lilliputian selves should we agree to share the occasion. Nevertheless it's bound to be more fun with Petrarch who plans to ascend Mount Ventoux in the 1330s and can't decide which friend to take. Eventually he'll make a touching choice.

If not touching, a few ahead are a little . . . touched. Or at least their views seem eccentric. Meet one who circles his room (under house arrest) and dreams he's circling the world; meet another who reckons the mineral riches of the earth are absorbed through the feet (he's leader of the Barefoot League); and another who 'breathed exclusively through his nostrils' for better health. The thing is, you can take something simple like walking and imbue it with a lot of conceits or rituals. Then it becomes an imaginative act, like questing for a pencil.

So, has anyone else escaped the desk? Definitely Charles Dickens. 'If I couldn't walk fast and far, I should just explode and perish,' he says – and often strode to the edges of London to shrug off insomnia. Many of his fictional characters went on foot, but it's an account of real-life 'tramps' that resonates. These people on the roads of the 1850s are a mixed lot, and find the going hard at times. Nevertheless the author is clearly with them: they are given names, trades, a dignity of sorts. Theirs is a sense of freedom when roaming between England's southern towns. And, as Petrarch would appreciate, a personal connection matters most: together they make up a 'tramp fellowship'.

Dickens's train of men, women and children walked from necessity, rarely for reasons of health, curiosity or creativity. The mass movements he describes – from which Hazlitt might run a mile – exist in many forms today. Picture refugees filing along mountain paths; political marchers claiming the streets; football crowds; festival strollers; charity hikers; shoppers. Everyone is on the move and usually it has to do with joining up, enjoying solidarity and communality as the miles pass.

This collection is bookended by solo strollers sharing the same habit. Kierkegaard has written about bringing 'bliss' home, the bliss that has intensified during his outings. But once home, if he meets another in sober mood the bliss will fade – and he will walk once more. Ditto Franz Kafka, fresh from a jaunt and apparently settled. Yet, as he's been:

sitting quietly at our table for so long that our going out would provoke general astonishment, when the stairwell is dark and the front gate is bolted, and when, in spite of it all, in a sudden access of restlessness, we get up, change into a jacket, and straightaway look ready to go out, explain that we are compelled to go out, and after a brief round of goodbyes actually do so . . .

It's a pity no word exists for the act of going out a second time. Kierkegaard should have found one for Kafka's later use. Anyway, if the walkers in *Beneath My Feet* tempt you to unlatch the door again today – that's good. With new reasons for setting off – for four hours, or fewer, if need be.

Happy strolling!

Postscript – I've been a bit critical about William Hazlitt, his tendency to bluster at times, and his solitariness. But he was a great pedestrian and did furnish the book with its lovely title, so let's thank him for that.

Ernest Delahaye

– Ready for Everything –

He had the strong and sinewy look of the determined and patient walker, who is always going off, his long legs moving quietly and very regularly, his head straight, his beautiful eyes fixed on the distance, and his face filled with a look of steady defiance, an air of expectation – ready for everything, without anger, without fear.

On Arthur Rimbaud, 1925

Frank Tatchell

– Few People Walk Well –

K eep a Regular Stride, rising on the balls of the toes and not turning the toes out too much: Rodin's statue of St John, in the Luxemburg, shows the correct way to have the feet. How few people know how to walk well. The secret is to let the shoulder opposite to the advancing foot swing well forward at each step.

From *The Happy Traveller*, 1925

Søren Aaby Kierkegaard

– I Walk for Health and Salvation –

D ear Jette,
Above all, do not lose your desire to walk: every day I walk myself into a state of well being and walk away from every illness. I have walked myself into my best thoughts, and I know of no thought so burdensome that one cannot walk away from it. Even if one were to walk for one's health and it were constantly one section ahead – I would still say walk! Besides, it is also apparent that in walking, one constantly gets as close to well-being as possible, even if one does not quite reach it – but by sitting still, and the more one sits still, the closer one comes to feeling ill. Health and salvation can only be found in motion. If anyone denies that motion exists, I do as Diogenes did, I walk. If anyone denies that health resides in motion, then I walk away from morbid objections. Thus if one keeps on walking, everything will be alright. And out in the country you have all the advantages; you do not risk being stopped before you are safe and happy outside your gate, nor do you run the risk of being intercepted on your way home. I remember exactly what happened to me a while ago and what has happened frequently since then. I had been walking for an hour and a half

and had done a great deal of thinking, and with the help of motion had become very agreeable person to myself. What bliss, and, as you may imagine, what care did I not take to bring my bliss home as safely as possible. Thus, I hurry along, with downcast eyes I steal through the streets, so to speak; confident that I am entitled to the sidewalk, I do not consider it necessary to look about at all (for thereby one is so easily intercepted, just as one is looking about in order to avoid) and thus hasten along the sidewalk with my bliss (for the ordinance forbidding one to carry anything on the sidewalk does not extend to bliss, which makes a person lighter) – and run directly into a man who is suffering from illness and who therefore with downcast eyes, defiant because of this illness, does not even think he must look about when he is not entitled to the sidewalk. I was stopped. It was quite an exalted gentleman who now honoured me with his conversation. Thus, all was lost. After the conversation ended, there was only one thing left to do, instead of going home, to go walking again.

Yours, S Kierkegaard.

From 'Letter to Henrietta Lund', 1847
(trans. Henrik Rosenmeier, 1978)

Nicholas Shakespeare

– I Walk Because Senses are Heightened –

Early one morning, just before Easter, I shook my two young sons awake and took them, still blinking, down to the nine mile beach that fringes the northern shore of Great Oyster Bay. The temperature was cool, there were no insects, the sun was not up yet. There had been a storm a few days before, but now the bay was calm.

Who walks at dawn?

Perhaps it takes a certain calmness of the soul, but a walk before sunrise contributes to a person's tranquility. I defy anyone to come out walking in the early hours and not feel something – 'If we walk on the sands of the sea, we shall taste the various qualities of the salts therein,' wrote the passionate tramper James Bain in 1914. It's not merely that your senses of taste and touch are heightened, but your senses to see, hear. At night the sound of tyres on the road is muffled, as if absorbed by the darkness. In the dawn, noises are crisper, carry further. And the stars shine brighter. I look up at the Milky Way, astonishingly luminescent, and remember how Richard Holmes compared this bucket of stars splashed across the sky to something indescribable, but affirming 'like falling upwards into someone's arms'. I nuture a ludicrous thought: if more people came out in the early morning, wouldn't there be less conflict in the world?

The moon has gone.

The colours seem opposite to what they were at dusk, as if put away at night and now unpacking for the day. As we walk barefoot on the sand, the cool sea boiling over our feet, I have a sense of the world beginning again; there's a furry glow behind the peninsula's dark silhouette, not an angry red, as at sunset, but the pastelly orange of a peach or cantaloupe. Light at dusk gathers all colours to the sinking sun, drawing them in; this morning I notice the colours expand and explore; fresh, clean, illuminating this pathway to the gods.

'Can we turn around now?' asks my eldest son, Max.

From *Dawnwalks*, 2015

Rebecca Solnit

– I Walk for Thoughts, Experiences, Arrivals –

I sat down one spring day to write about walking and stood up again, because a desk is no place to think on the large scale. In a headland just north of the Golden Gate Bridge studded with abandoned military fortifications, I went out walking up a valley and along a ridgeline, then down to the Pacific. Spring had come after an unusually wet winter, and the hills had turned that riotous, exuberant green I forget and re-discover every year. Through the new growth poked grass from the year before, bleached from the summer gold to an ashen grey by the rain, part of the subtler palette of the rest of the year. Henry David Thoreau, who walked more vigorously than me on the other side of the continent, wrote of the local, 'An absolutely new prospect is a great happiness, and I can still get this any afternoon. Two or three hours' walking will carry me to as strange a county as I expect ever to see. A single farmhouse which I had not seen before is sometimes as good as the dominions of the King of Dahomey. There is in fact a sort of harmony discoverable between the capabilities of the landscape within a circle of ten miles' radius, or the limits of an afternoon walk, and the threescore years and ten of human life. It will never become quite familiar to you.'

These linked paths and roads form a circuit of about six miles that I began hiking ten years ago to walk off my angst during a difficult year. I kept coming back to this route for respite from my work and for my work too, because thinking is generally thought of as doing nothing in a production-orientated culture, and doing nothing is hard to do. It's best done by disguising it as doing something, and the something closest to doing nothing is walking. Walking itself is the intentional act closest to the unwilled rhythms of the body, to breathing and the beating of the heart. It strikes a delicate balance between working and idling, being and doing. It is a bodily labor that produces nothing but thoughts, experiences, arrivals. After all those years of walking to work out other things, it made sense to come back to work close to home, in Thoreau's sense, and to think about walking.

Walking, ideally, is a state in which the mind, the body, and the world are aligned, as though they were three characters finally in conversation together, three notes suddenly making a chord. Walking allows us to be in our bodies and in the world without being made busy by them. It leaves us free to think without being wholly lost in our thoughts. I wasn't sure whether I was to soon or too late for the purple lupine that can be so spectacular in these headlands, but milkmaids were growing on the shady side of the road on the way to the trail, and they recalled the hillsides of my childhood that first bloomed every year with an extravagance of these white flowers. Black butterflies fluttered around me, tossed along by wind and wings, and they called up another era of my past. Moving on foot seems to make it easier to move in time; the mind wanders from plans to recollections to observations.

From *Wanderlust*, 2001

Lucy Hughes-Hallett

– The Dog and I –

T wice or three times a week the dog and I get up early to walk around a nineteenth-century cemetery in north London. I'm not going to name it. To do so might jeopardise the benign conspiracy between those of us who frequent the place, and its keepers, who pretend to be as blind as we are to the signs at the entrance about dogs and leads.

The cemetery is shaped like a round-shouldered coffin, which is fitting. It reminds me of a game from my childhood called Bagatelle. At the straight end of the Bagatelle board (which was more like a wooden tray) there was a kind of trigger, with which one shot a glass marble into a thicket of pins. It was a tedious game. When (and if) it was played at the Chateau de Bagatelle in the last days before the French Revolution, I guess it might have been enlivened by the wagering of stupendous sums of money.

I digress. This happens a lot. Part of the pleasure of walking is the way it sets your mind free to wander. Once we reach the cemetery my dog, who is a large hairy pointer called Kilburn, wanders too.

Our cemetery is not one of London's great cities of the dead, like Highgate or Kensal Green. It is only a few acres. To get a proper walk you have to criss-cross it repeatedly, or circumnavigate it several times.

When it was first laid out it must have been forbiddingly prim. At its northern end the geometry of concentric semi-circular paths is still clear. Here there is tarmac, and the new graves are mostly made of black marble with a shine designed to last until the last trump, however long that may be delayed. Further from the entrance, though, pebbled paths are invaded by moss and flowery weeds. Shrubs planted a century ago, as neat knee-high mounds of green, are now house-high, each sprawling over the grave it was designed to adorn, and several of its neighbours too. Gravestones prop each other up. Stone crucifixes lie prone beneath the cow-parsley. There are grassy raised areas like the bases of pyramids. Are they hillocks of the piled-up dead? Maybe, but as I walk over them now, in early spring, they are starred with raggedy white anemones. Later the foxgloves will take over.

Among the early-morning walkers there are purposeful ones who hurry around the periphery with earphones in. There are pairs of friends who pace up and down the avenue of venerable plane trees. There is an open space where dog-owners stand like a clump of maypoles, discussing ailments and house-moves while their dogs run rings around them. We just stroll.

To Kilburn, a walk isn't exercise. It's a party, a

chance to find other beings with whom to perform clumsy, earth-bound pirouettes, or wrestle, or fall in love. He has a far wider acquaintance than I do. He comes here with his walker, later in the day, when I'm working. He has a private life. 'It's Kilburn, isn't it?' strangers say to me, as he whirls their spaniel or labradoodle off for a polka around the tombstones. Failing dogs, there are humans. Failing humans, there are squirrels, but they have a frustrating ability to dematerialise when in proximity to a tree. It never occurs to Kilburn to look up.

While he roams, I amble after him, and my mind, only newly awake, rambles as inconsequentially. Walkers, wrote Henry Thoreau, should imitate the camel 'the only beast which ruminates when walking'. Thoreau had to have his daily walk – without it he felt rust enveloping him. There was a Scottish clerk with the East India company known as 'Walking' Stewart. In the 1790s he walked all the way home from Madras, with side-trips into Abyssinia and Russia along the way – which makes Patrick Leigh-Fermor's much written-up walk to Istanbul seem paltry stuff. I'm not in competition with such marathon-men. What I like is that Thomas de Quincey (himself a great one for walking) got to know Walking Stewart when he had settled his old bones in London. He records that Stewart went each morning to St James's Park. There he would play his bagpipes. Or he would just sit, says de Quincey, 'in contemplative ease amongst the cows, inhaling their balmy breath and pursuing his philosophic reveries'. My mind-wanderings are seldom philosophic, but reveries – dreamy meanderings – they certainly are.

Some of the time I'm reminiscing. I've been coming to the cemetery for years now and there are memories imprinted in the turf. Beneath this crooked pine tree I sheltered from the rain with my daughters, when they were small enough to walk into the cave it makes without bending their heads. 'It's like being a badger,' one of them said. By this holly-bush I took a call from my father's carer telling me he'd had his last fall. But I'm not seeking out the past. A lot of the time I'm observing passively. Reading my mind would be as dull as reading a shopping list. 'Primroses!' I think. Or 'Mud'. Or 'Parakeets'. But then a digression begins. Like that trip to ancien regime Bagatelle, it's often triggered by a name.

Near to the entrance, stands an imposing monument from the 1930s. A classically draped lady weeping over a veiled urn. It's the tomb of Garibaldi Stephenson, born in 1864. He must have been named in honour of the visit to London that year of Italy's nationalist hero. When the great Garibaldi came to London, tens of thousands of enthusiasts blocked the streets for hours, squashed-fly (or Garibaldi) biscuits went into production, and the Stephenson baby was saddled with his outlandish name. What did his friends call him, I wonder? Garry? What else is Garry short for? Gareth? Are most Garrys Welsh, then? See what I mean by digressing. This is the way my walking thoughts drift.

Repeatedly, they are tugged back to the present by the cemetery's beauty. In winter the leafless plane trees veil the skies with black lace and the new-risen sun is an incandescent pink. Summer and autumn bring buttercups or berries, but now it's spring. Dainty miniature daffodils have spread outside the stone surrounds of the grave in which they were planted decades ago, and naturalised themselves. An ornamental plum tree has cracked a tombstone from side to side, and blossoms above it. I know the names of very few of my fellow walkers (although I know their dogs' names) but we all know each other well enough to remark what a wonderful year it is for violets. Every year, we say this.

So there's new life, and, given where we are, there's death to think about too. Or more particularly, mourning, and memorialising. It's rum what people think fit to put on gravestones. Names, and dates of birth and death, of course. Sir Thomas Browne, the seventeenth-century essayist, wrote that 'to subsist in bones, and be but pyramidally extant, is a fallacy in duration'. A monument must bear a name, but Browne wanted more. 'Who cares to subsist like Achilles' horses in Homer, under naked nominations, without deserts and noble acts, which are the balsam of our memories?' There are very few deserts or noble acts recorded on the gravestones Kilburn and I pass by. There are a pair of brothers, as competitive in death as one imagines they were in life, whose pink granite slabs lie side by side, proclaiming their professional achievements. One was President of the Positivist Society. He died in 1915, in the middle of a war that must have made positive thinking hard. The other was Assistant Master at Marlborough College.

But these are exceptions. The great majority of the dead are defined only by their relationships. By the new graves there are foot-high words worked with flowers and shiny cellophane ribbon – seldom the dead person's name. Instead Grandad, Dad, Nan, My Wife. On the tombstones – 'My darling husband'; 'Our dear son'; 'A fonder mother and more loving wife/Ne'er breathed the breath of mortal life.' Living, these people must have had secret thoughts, lives that belonged to them as individuals, but now their relatives lay claim to them. From the 1850s, when this cemetery was established, right up to the present, the message is constant. 'The lord takes those we love from our homes but never from our hearts.' Through these dutiful descriptions sounds a childish plea for possession. She's mine. He's ours. 'God Knows Best' reads one tomb, but these mourners aren't going to stand aside and abdicate their claims to Him.

'I always thought I'd like my own tombstone to be blank,' said Andy Warhol, who wasn't much of a family man. 'No epitaph, and no name. Well, actually, I'd like it to say "figment".' Warhol was the figment of his own imagination – his public persona was his own brilliant creation. These dead Londoners are now the figments of their sorrowing relatives' imaginations. 'Our fathers find their graves in our short memories,' wrote Thomas Browne. And who really knows their parents? 'Not in front of the children' was a constant refrain of my childhood. People have lives their families know nothing of. But here complex human beings are reduced, in love and duty, to one-word job descriptions – 'Nan' 'Grandad' 'Mum'.

Kilburn is fond of mourners. I'm ready to drag him away from anyone sitting solitary on a bench, contemplating a grave. But some call him. He puts his head on their laps (he's tall enough to do so without jumping up) and waits to have his ears fondled. Then he's off again, skidding dangerously over the flat stone slabs, playing bending races around the standing tombs.

When we leave, stepping out into the din of modern London, there's a moment of jarring re-adjustment. The poet Gabriele d'Annunzio used cemeteries as an image of the rapt state of concentration in which he wrote. Breaking from his work, he said was like being turned out into a road bordering a cemetery wall, and glimpsing above it trees, and the heads of the tallest statues, while being shut out of that mysterious space in which inspiration came.

Kilburn and I go home at a brisk pace for breakfast. We pass the house where Kilburn's friend the golden retriever lives (he always has to sniff the door). We pass the corner shop where vegetables are displayed in shiny aluminium bowls. We pass the little girls in headscarves going in a walking crocodile to the Islamic school. We're back in the land of the living, and glad to be there, ready to begin the day. But our early morning digression into reverie has been precious.

As Thoreau knew, all that sauntering and ruminating has its hidden purpose: 'The Saunterer is no more vagrant than the meandering river, which is all the while sedulously seeking the shortest course to the sea.'

From *Dawnwalks*, 2016

Chevalier de la Tocnaye

– I Wanted for Nothing –

At Limerick I was obliged entirely to renew my wardrobe, which at the time of my departure from Dublin consisted only of my clothes and what could be contained in two silk stockings from which I had cut the feet. Although my baggage was inconsiderable, I wanted for nothing, and had the means of appearing in society as well dressed as others.

For the information of future travellers on foot, it is my pleasure here to give details of my complete equipment.

A powder bag made out of a woman's glove.

A razor.

Thread.

Needles.

Scissors.

A comb, carried in one of a pair of dress shoes.

A pair of silk stockings.

Breeches, fine enough to be, when folded, not bigger than a fist.

Two very fine shirts.

Three cravats.

Three handkerchiefs.

The clothes in which I travelled.

The sundries I divided in three, two lots going into the silk stockings which served as bags, the third packet contained my shoes. I had six pockets: in three of them were stowed the packets, as described, when I was about to enter a house of consequence; but as this packing would be very inconvenient while walking, I was accustomed, on the road, to tie my three packets in a handkerchief and carry the load over my shoulder at the end of my sword-stick, on which I had grafted an umbrella which excited, everywhere, curiosity, and made the girls laugh – I can't tell why. The remaining pockets were reserved for letters, my pocket-book, and ordinary uses.

The persons who received me, and whose offers of linen I always refused, were much astonished to see me reappear in the drawing-room in silk stockings and powder as if I had travelled with considerable baggage at my ease, and in a fine carriage.

Hey! Mr Sterne, what do you think of the wardrobe with which I travelled for six solid months? – putting up at the very best houses. My portmanteau was as good as yours, I trow.

From 'A Frenchman's Walk Through Ireland', 1796
(trans. John Stevenson, 1917)

John Hillaby

– Barefoot through Bogs and Only a Pair of Shorts –

F ootwear is tricky. I treat my feet like premature twins. The moment I feel even a slight twinge of discomfort I stop and put it right. Most people advocate stout boots and thick socks. I know of nothing more uncomfortable. They give you a leaden, non-springy stride. You can't trot along in boots. I bought two pairs, broke them in and eventually threw them aside. On a trip across the desert some years ago, I wore tennis shoes, but these I found, are useless in Britain, for they become sodden. After trying various kinds of shoes, I settled for an expensive Italian pair with light commando-type soles. They weighed about fifteen ounces each and, when oiled, fitted me like gloves. I had no trouble with shoes. Certainly not from blisters, although in the last stages of the journey some of my toenails dropped off. In places I went barefoot through bogs, and on warm days in deserted country I sometimes wore only a pair of shorts.

From *Journey Through Britain*, 1968

A. H. Sidgwick

– The Coat will go Back to the Cupboard –

B oots have grown limp; clothes have settled natural skin-like rumples: the stick is warm and smooth to our touch: the map slips easily in and out of pockets, lucubrated like dog's ears: every article in the knapsack has found its natural place, and the whole has settled onto our shoulders. The equipment is no longer an armour of which we are conscious. At the start this coat was a glorious thing to face the world in: now it is merely an outer skin. At the start this stick was mine: now it is myself.

When it is all over the coat will go back to the cupboard and the curved suspensor and the shirts and stockings will go to the wash, to resume conventional form and texture, and take their place in the humdrum world. But in the darkest hours of urban depression I will sometimes take out the dog-eared map and dream awhile of more spacious days; and perhaps a dried blade of grass will fall out of it to remind me that once I was a free man on the hills.

From *Walking Essays*, 1912

– And I Walk for a Secret Feeling of Poetic Capacity –

F our hours would be quite sufficient for the execution of the enterprise, as I only intended to make a short excursion round my room.

If my first journey lasted 42 days, that was because I was unable to shorten it. I did not intend to travel in a carriage as before, feeling sure that a pedestrian sees much that is missed by he who takes post horses. I therefore resolved to travel alternately, or according to circumstances, on foot or on horseback: a new method which I have not yet made known, and whose usefulness will be soon seen. Lastly, I determined to take notes on the road, and to write down my observations as they occurred to me, so as not to forget anything. In order to carry out my plan systematically, and to give it a further chance of success, I thought I ought to begin with a dedication, written in verse, to make it more interesting. But two difficulties occurred to me and nearly made me give up the idea, notwithstanding its apparent advantages. The first was to know to whom to address the dedication, and the second was how to make verses. After having thought it over, I saw that reason demanded that I should write my dedication first and then consider to whom it was best suited. I set to work at once and laboured for more than an hour to find a rhyme to the first line I had written, and which I wished to preserve, as it seemed to me rather good. I then remembered that I had read somewhere that Pope never composed anything interesting save after repeating many lines aloud and moving rapidly about his study to excite his energy. I at once tried to imitate him. I took the poems of Ossian and repeated them aloud, pacing my room to arouse my enthusiasm. I perceived that this method certainly warmed my imagination, and gave me a secret feeling of poetic capacity, which I should have made use of to compose my dedication, had I not forgotten the obliquity of the roof of my room, whose acute angle prevented my forehead from going as far as my feet in the direction I had taken. I struck so hard against this confounded wall, that the roof of the house was shaken: the sparrows that slept under the eaves fled, filled with terror, and the concussion sent me fully three steps back.

Whilst I was thus walking about to excite my imagination, a young and pretty woman who lodged below, astonished at the noise I was making, and thinking, perhaps, I was giving a dance in my room, dispatched her husband to find out the reason of the disturbance. I was still confused with the blow I had experienced when the door opened. An elderly man, with a melancholy face, put in his head, and gave an inquisitive glance round the room. When the surprise of finding me alone allowed him to speak, he said: 'My wife has a headache. Sir. Allow me to call your attention . . .' I interrupted him at once, and my style reflected the height my thoughts had risen to: 'Respectable messenger of my lovely neighbour,' said I in the language of the bards, 'why do thine eyes sparkle beneath thy bushy eyebrows, like two meteors in the black forest of Cromba? Thy lovely mate is a ray of light, and I would die a thousand deaths ere I troubled her repose; but thine aspect, oh respectable messenger, thine aspect is dark as the furthermost vault of the Cavern of Camora, when the gathered stormclouds darken the face of night, and lower over the silent plains of Morven.'

The neighbour, who had apparently never read the poems of Ossian, mistook this fit of enthusiasm for a fit of lunacy and seemed much embarrassed. Having no intention to offend him, I offered him a chair, and begged him to be seated. But I perceived that he softly withdrew, making the sign of the Cross, and murmuring: 'E matto, per Baccho, è matto!' – he's mad by Bacchus, he's mad.

From 'A Nocturnal Expedition around My Room', 1825
(trans. Edmund Goldsmid, 1886)

John Muir

– Roasted in an Oven –

I n the great Central Valley of California there are only two seasons – spring and summer. The spring begins with the first rainstorm, which usually falls in November. In a few months the wonderful flowery vegetation is in full bloom, and by the end of May it is dead and dry and crisp, as if every plant had been roasted in an oven.

Then the lolling, panting flocks and herds are driven to the high, cool, green pastures of the Sierra. I was longing for the mountains about this time, but money was scarce and I couldn't see how a bread supply was to be kept up. While I was anxiously brooding on the bread problem, so troublesome to wanderers, and trying to believe that I might learn to live like the wild animals, gleaning nourishment here and there from seeds, berries, etc., sauntering and climbing in joyful independence of money or baggage, Mr Delaney, a sheep-owner, for whom I had worked a few weeks, called on me, and offered to engage me to go with his shepherd and flock to the headwaters of the Merced and Tuolumne rivers – the very region I had most in mind. I was in the mood to accept work of any kind that would take me into the mountains whose treasures I had tasted last summer in the Yosemite region.

I was fortunate in getting a fine St Bernard dog for a companion. His master, a hunter with whom I was slightly acquainted, came to me as soon as he heard that I was going to spend the summer in the Sierra and begged me to take his favorite dog, Carlo, with me, for he feared that if he were compelled to stay all summer on the plains the fierce heat might be the death of him. 'I think I can trust you to be kind to him,' he said, 'and I am sure he will be good to you.' Calling him by name, I asked him if he was willing to go with me. He looked me in the face with eyes expressing wonderful intelligence, then turned to his master, and after permission was given by a wave of the hand toward me and a farewell patting caress, he quietly followed me as if he perfectly understood all that had been said and had known me always.

June 3, 1869. – This morning provisions, camp-kettles, blankets, plant-press, etc., were packed on two horses, the flock headed for the tawny foothills, and away we sauntered in a cloud of dust: Mr Delaney, bony and tall, with sharply hacked profile like Don Quixote, leading the pack-leading the pack-horses, Billy, the proud shepherd, a Chinaman and a Digger Indian to assist in driving for the first few days in the brushy foothills, and myself with notebook tied to my belt.

The home ranch from which we set out is on the

south side of the Tuolumne River near French Bar, where the foothills of metamorphic gold-bearing slates dip below the stratified deposits of the Central Valley. We had not gone more than a mile before some of the old leaders of the flock showed by the eager, inquiring way they ran and looked ahead that they were thinking of the high pastures they had enjoyed last summer. Soon the whole flock seemed to be hopefully excited, the mothers calling their lambs, the lambs replying in tones wonderfully human, their fondly quavering calls interrupted now and then by hastily snatched mouthfuls of withered grass. Amid all this seeming babel of baas as they streamed over the hills every mother and child recognized each other's voice. In case a tired lamb, half asleep in the smothering dust, should fail to answer, its mother would come running back through the flock toward the spot whence its last response was heard, and refused to be comforted until she found it, the one of a thousand, though to our eyes and ears all seemed alike.

The flock traveled at the rate of about a mile an hour, outspread in the form of an irregular triangle, about a hundred yards wide at the base, and a hundred and fifty yards long, with a crooked, ever-changing point made up of the strongest foragers, called the 'leaders', which, with the most active of those scattered along the ragged sides of the 'main body', hastily explored nooks in the rocks and bushes for grass and leaves; the lambs and feeble old mothers dawdling in the rear were called the 'tail end'.

About noon the heat was hard to bear; the poor sheep panted pitifully and tried to stop in the shade of every tree they came to, while we gazed with eager longing through the dim burning glare toward the snowy mountains and streams, though not one was in sight. The landscape is only wavering foothills roughened here and there with bushes and trees and outcropping masses of slate. The trees, mostly the blue oak (*Quercus Douglasii*), are about thirty to forty feet high, with pale blue-green leaves and white bark, sparsely planted on the thinnest soil or in crevices of rocks beyond the reach of grass fires. The slates in many places rise abruptly through the tawny grass in sharp lichen-covered slabs like tombstones in deserted burying-grounds. With the exception of the oak and four or five species of manzanita and ceanothus, the vegetation of the foothills is mostly the same as that of the plains. I saw this region in the early spring, when it was a charming landscape garden full of birds and bees and flowers. Now the scorching weather makes everything dreary. The ground is full of cracks, lizards glide about on the rocks, and ants in amazing numbers, whose tiny sparks of life only burn the brighter with the heat, fairly quiver with unquenchable energy as they run in long lines to fight and gather food. How it comes that they do not dry to a crisp in a few seconds' exposure to such sun-fire is marvelous. A few rattlesnakes lie coiled in out-of-the-way places, but are seldom seen. Magpies and crows, usually so noisy, are silent now, standing in mixed flocks on the ground beneath the best shade trees, with bills wide open and wings drooped, too breathless to speak; the quails also are trying to keep in the shade about the few tepid alkaline water holes; cottontail rabbits are running from shade to shade among the ceanothus brush, and occasionally the long-eared hare is seen cantering gracefully across the wider openings.

After a short noon rest in a grove, the poor dust-choked flock was again driven ahead over the brushy hills, but the dim roadway we had been following faded away just where it was most needed, compelling us to stop to look about us and get our bearings. The Chinaman seemed to think we were lost, and chattered in pidgin English concerning the abundance of 'litty stick' (chaparral), while the Indian silently scanned the billowy ridges and gulches for openings. Pushing through the thorny jungle, we at length discovered a road trending toward Coulterville, which we followed until an hour before sunset, when we reached a dry ranch and camped for the night.

Camping in the foothills with a flock of sheep is simple and easy, but far from pleasant. The sheep were allowed to pick what they could find in the neighborhood until after sunset, watched by the shepherd, while the others gathered wood, made a fire, cooked, unpacked and fed the horses, etc. About dusk the weary sheep were gathered on the highest open spot near camp, where they willingly bunched close together, and after each mother had found her lamb and suckled it, all lay down and required no attention until morning.

Supper was announced by the call, 'Grub!' Each with a tin plate helped himself direct from the pots and pans while chatting about such camp studies as sheep feed, mines, coyotes, bears, or adventures during the memorable gold days of paydirt. The Indian kept in the background, saying never a word, as if he belonged to another species. The meal finished, the dogs were fed, the smokers smoked by the fire, and under the influences of fullness and tobacco the calm that settled on their faces seemed almost divine, something like the mellow meditative glow portrayed on the countenances of saints. Then suddenly, as if awakening from a dream, each with a sigh or a grunt knocked the ashes out of his pipe, yawned, gazed at the fire a few moments, said, 'Well, I believe I'll turn in,' and straightway vanished beneath his blankets.

June 4. – The camp was astir at day break; coffee, bacon, and beans formed the breakfast, followed by quick dishwashing and packing. A general bleating began about sunrise. As soon as a mother ewe arose, her lamb came bounding and bunting for its breakfast, and after the thousand youngsters had been suckled the flock began to nibble and spread. The restless wethers with ravenous appetites were the first to move, but dared not go far from the main body. Billy and the Indian and the Chinaman kept them headed along the weary road, and allowed them to pick up what little they could find on a breadth of about a quarter of a mile. But as several flocks had already gone ahead of us, scarce a leaf, green or dry, was left; therefore the starving flock had to be hurried on over the bare, hot hills to the nearest of the green pastures, about twenty or thirty miles from here.

The pack-animals were led by Don Quixote, a heavy rifle over his shoulder intended for bears and wolves. This day has been as hot and dusty as the first, leading over gently sloping brown hills, with mostly the same vegetation, excepting the strange-looking Sabine pine (*Pinus Sabiniana*), which here forms small groves or is scattered among the blue oaks. The trunk divides at a height of fifteen or twenty feet into two or more stems, outleaning or nearly upright, with many straggling branches and long gray needles, casting but little shade. In general appearance this tree looks more like a palm than a pine. The cones are about six or seven inches long, about five in diameter, very heavy, and last long after they fall, so that the ground beneath the trees is covered with them. They make fine resiny, light-giving campfires, next to ears of Indian corn the most beautiful fuel I've ever seen. The nuts, the Don tells me, are gathered in large quantities by the Digger Indians for food. They are about as large and hard-shelled as hazelnuts, – food and fire fit for the gods from the same fruit.

June 5. – This morning a few hours after setting out with the crawling sheep-cloud, we gained the summit of the first well-defined bench on the mountain-flank at Pino Blanco. The Sabine pines interest me greatly. They are so airy and strangely palm-like I was eager to sketch them, and was in a fever of excitement without accomplishing much. I managed to halt long enough, however, to make a tolerably fair sketch of Pino Blanco peak from the southwest side, where there is a small field and vineyard irrigated by a stream that makes a pretty fall on its way down a gorge by the roadside. After gaining the open summit of this first bench, feeling the natural exhilaration due to the slight elevation of a thousand feet or so, and the hopes excited concerning the Horseshoe Bend, Merced River outlook to be obtained, a magnificent section of the Merced Valley at what is called Horseshoe Bend came full in sight, – a glorious wilderness that seemed to be calling with a thousand songful voices. Bold, down-sweeping slopes, feathered with pines and clumps of manzanita with sunny, open spaces between them, make up most of the foreground; the middle and background present fold beyond fold of finely modeled hills and ridges rising into mountain-like masses in the distance, all covered with a shaggy growth of chaparral, mostly adenostoma, planted so marvelously close and even that it looks like soft, rich plush without a single tree or bare spot. As far as the eye can reach it extends, a heaving, swelling sea of green as regular and continuous as that produced by the heaths of Scotland. The sculpture of the landscape is as striking in its main lines as in its lavish richness of detail; a grand congregation of massive heights with the river shining between, each carved into smooth, graceful folds without leaving a single rocky angle exposed, as if the delicate fluting and ridging fashioned out of metamorphic slates had been carefully sandpapered. The whole landscape showed design, like man's noblest sculptures. How wonderful the power of its beauty! Gazing awe-stricken, I might have left everything for it. Glad, endless work would then be mine tracing the forces that have brought forth its features, its rocks and plants and animals and glorious weather. Beauty beyond thought everywhere, beneath, above, made and being made forever. I gazed and gazed and longed and admired until the dusty sheep and packs were far out of sight, made hurried notes and a sketch, though there was no need of either, for the colors and lines and expression of this divine landscape-countenance are so burned into mind and heart they surely can never grow dim. The evening of this charmed day is cool, calm, cloudless, and full of a kind of lightning I have never seen before – white glowing cloud-shaped masses down among the trees and bushes, like quick-throbbing fireflies in the Wisconsin meadows rather than the so-called 'wild fire'. The spreading hairs of the horses' tails and sparks from our blankets show how highly charged the air is.

From *My First Summer in the Sierra*, 1911

James Leith Macbeth Bain

– Our Feet Absorb the World's Goodness –

All the parts of the earth's surface on which we tread will fulfill a particular service of life for the health of the body. Thus if we walk on the young and living grass we shall receive its fresh and living – yet soothing – virtue. If we walk on the mountain turf, not in the sun's rays, we shall receive the very strength of the mountain.

If we walk in the pine wood, an oak wood, a birch or larch wood we would surely receive of the peculiar virtues of these fragrant creatures of Life. If we walk on the sands of the sea we shall taste the various qualities of the salt therein. If we walk on dry clay or mud we shall at once recognize that the nutrition thus imparted to our nerval body is finer or more comforting than that conveyed through rough sand or fine shingle.

From *The Barefoot League*, 1914

Mary Kingsley

– In Stinging Rain –

S eptember 26th. – The weather is undecided and so am I, for I feel doubtful about going on in this weather, but I do not like to give up the peak after going through so much for it. The boys being dry and warm with the fires have forgotten their troubles. However, I settle in my mind to keep on, and ask for volunteers to come with me, and Bum, the head man, and Xenia announce their willingness. I put two tins of meat and a bottle of Herr Liebert's beer into the little wooden box, and insist on both men taking a blanket apiece, much to their disgust, and before six o'clock we are off over the crater plain. It is a broken bit of country with rock mounds sparsely overgrown with tufts of grass, and here and there are patches of boggy land, not real bog, but damp places where grow little clumps of rushes, and here and there among the rocks sorely-afflicted shrubs of broom, and the yellow-flowered shrub I have mentioned before, and quantities of very sticky heather, feeling when you catch hold of it as if it had been covered with syrup. One might fancy the entire race of shrubs was dying out; for one you see partially alive there are twenty skeletons which fall to pieces as you brush past them.

It is downhill the first part of the way, that is to say, the trend of the land is downhill, for be it down or up, the details of it are rugged mounds and masses of burnt-out lava rock. It is evil going, but perhaps not quite so evil as the lower hillocks of the great wall where the rocks are hidden beneath long slippery grass. We wind our way in between the mounds, or clamber over them, or scramble along their sides impartially. The general level is then flat, and then comes a rise towards the peak wall, so we steer N.N.E. until we strike the face of the peak, and then commence a stiff rough climb.

We keep as straight as we can, but get driven at an angle by the strange ribs of rock which come straight down. These are most tiresome to deal with, getting worse the higher we go, and so rotten and weather-eaten are they that they crumble into dust and fragments under our feet. Head man gets half a dozen falls, and when we are about three parts of the way up Xenia gives in. The cold and the climbing are too much for him, so I make him wrap himself up in his blanket, which he is glad enough of now, and shelter in a depression under one of the many rock ridges, and Head man and I go on. When we are some 600 feet higher the iron-grey mist comes curling and waving round the rocks above us, like some savage monster defending them from intruders, and I again debate whether I was justified in risking the men, for it is a risk for them at this low temperature, with the evil weather I know, and they do not know, is coming on. But still we have food and blankets with us enough for them, and the camp in the plain below they can reach all right, if the worst comes to the worst; and for myself – well – that's my own affair, and no one will be a ha'porth the worse if I am dead in an hour. So I hitch myself on to the rocks, and take bearings, particularly bearings of Xenia's position, who, I should say, has got a tin of meat and a flask of rum with him.

And then Bum, the head man, decides to fail for the third time to reach the peak, and I leave him wrapped in his blanket with the bag of provisions, and go on alone and soon find myself at the head of a rock ridge in a narrowish depression.

I can see three distinctly high cones before me, and then a sheet of blinding, stinging rain. I make my way towards a peak which I soon see, so I angle off and go up to the left, and after a desperate fight reach the cairn – only, alas! to find a hurricane raging and not a ten yards' view to be had in any direction. Near the cairn on the ground are several bottles, some of which the energetic German officers, I suppose, had emptied in honour of their achievement, an achievement I bow down before, for their pluck and strength had taken them here in a shorter time by far than mine. I do not meddle with anything, save to take a few specimens and to put a few more rocks on the cairn.

The weather grows worse every minute, and no sign of any clearing shows in the indigo sky.

Verily I am no mountaineer, for there is in me no exultation, but only a deep disgust because the weather has robbed me of my main object in coming here, namely to get a good view and an idea of the way the unexplored mountain range behind Calabar trends. I took my chance and it failed, so there's nothing to complain about.

Comforting myself with these reflections, I start down to find Bum, and do so neatly, and then together we scramble down carefully among the rotten black rocks, intent on finding Xenia.

The scene is very grand. At one minute we can see nothing save the black rocks and cinders under foot; the next one direction, now in another, showing us always the same wild scene of great black cliffs, rising in jagged peaks and walls around and above us. I think this walled cauldron we had just left is really the highest crater on Mungo.

We soon become anxious about Xenia, for this is a fearfully easy place to lose a man in such weather. But I observe a doll-sized figure, standing on one leg taking on or off its trousers – our lost Xenia, beyond a shadow of a doubt, and we go down direct to him.

When we reach him we halt, and I give the two men one of the tins of meat, and take another and the bottle of beer myself, and then make a hasty sketch of the great crater plain below us.

At the further edge of the plain a great white cloud is coming up from below, which argues badly for our trip down the great wall to the forest camp, which I am anxious to reach before nightfall.

While I am sitting waiting for the men to finish their meal, I feel a chill at my back, as if some cold thing had settled there, and turning round, see a mist from the summit above coming in a wall down towards us. These mists up here, as far as my experience goes, are always preceded by a strange breath of ice-cold air – not necessarily a wind.

Bum then draws my attention to a strange funnel-shaped thing coming down from the clouds to the north. A big waterspout, I presume. It seems to be moving rapidly N.E., and I profoundly hope it will hold that course, for we have quite as much as we can manage with the ordinary rain-water supply on this mountain, without having waterspouts to deal with.

We start off down the mountain as rapidly as we can. Xenia is very done up, and Head man comes perilously near breaking his neck by frequent falls among the rocks. My unlucky boots are cut through and through by the latter. When we get down towards the big crater plain, it is a race between us and the pursuing mist as to who shall reach the camp first, and the mist wins. But we have just time to make out the camp's exact position before it closes round us, so we reach it without any real difficulty. When we get there, about one o'clock, I find the men have kept the fires alight and Cook is asleep before one of them with another conflagration smouldering in his hair. I get him to make me tea, while the others pack up as quickly as possible, and by two we are all off on our way down to the forest camp.

From *Travels in West Africa*, 1897

Henry David Thoreau

– Through Fields of Snow –

We sleep, and at length awake to the still reality of a winter morning. The snow lies warm as cotton or down upon the windowsill; the broadened sash and frosted panes admit a dim and private light, which enhances the snug cheer within. The stillness of the morning is impressive. The floor creaks under our feet as we move toward the window to look abroad through some clear space over the fields. We see the roofs stand under their snow burden. From the eaves and fences hang stalactites of snow, and in the yard stand stalagmites covering some concealed core. The trees and shrubs rear white arms to the sky on every side; and where were walls and fences, we see fantastic forms stretching in frolic gambols across the dusky landscape, as if Nature had strewn her fresh designs over the fields by night as models for man's art.

Silently we unlatch the door, letting the drift fall in, and step abroad to face the cutting air. Already the stars have lost some of their sparkle, and a dull, leaden mist skirts the horizon. A lurid brazen light in the east proclaims the approach of day, while the western landscape is dim and spectral still, and clothed in a sombre Tartarean light, like the shadowy realms. They are Infernal sounds only that you hear, the crowing of cocks, the barking of dogs, the chopping of wood, the lowing of kine, all seem to come from Pluto's barnyard and beyond the Styx, not for any melancholy they suggest, but their twilight bustle is too solemn and mysterious for earth. The recent tracks of the fox or otter, in the yard, remind us that each hour of the night is crowded with events, and the primeval nature is still working and making tracks in the snow. Opening the gate, we tread briskly along the lone country road, crunching the dry and crisped snow under our feet, or aroused by the sharp, clear creak of the woodshed, just starting for the distant market, from the early farmer's door, where it has lain the summer long, dreaming amid the chips and stubble; while far through the drifts and powdered windows we see the farmer's early candle, like a paled star, emitting a lonely beam, as if some severe virtue were at its matins there. And one by one the smokes begin to ascend from the chimneys amid the trees and snows.

We hear the sound of woodchopping at the farmers' doors, far over the frozen earth, the baying of the house dog, and the distant clarion of the cock, though the thin and frosty air conveys only the finer particles of sound to our ears, with short and sweet vibrations, as the waves subside soonest on the purest and lightest liquids, in which gross substances sink to the bottom. They come clear and bell-like, and from a greater distance in the horizon, as if there were fewer impediments than in summer to make them faint and ragged. The ground is sonorous, like seasoned wood, and even the ordinary rural sounds are melodious, and the jingling of the ice on the trees is sweet and liquid. There is the least possible moisture in the atmosphere, all being dried up or congealed, and it is of such extreme tenuity and elasticity that it becomes a source of delight. The withdrawn and tense sky seems groined like the aisles of a cathedral, and the polished air sparkles as if there were crystals of ice floating in it. As they who have resided in Greenland tell us that when it freezes 'the sea smokes like burning turf-land, and a fog or mist arises, called frost-smoke,' which 'cutting smoke frequently raises blisters on the face and hands, and is very pernicious to the health.' But this pure, stinging cold is an elixir to the lungs, and not so much a frozen mist as a crystallized midsummer haze, refined and purified by cold.

The sun at length rises through the distant woods, as if with the faint clashing, swinging sound of cymbals, melting the air with his beams, and with such rapid steps the morning travels, that already his rays are gilding the distant western mountains. Meanwhile we step hastily along through the powdery snow, warmed by an inward heat, enjoying an Indian summer still, in the increased glow of thought and feeling. Probably if our lives were more conformed to nature, we should not need to defend ourselves against her heats and colds, but find her our constant nurse and friend, as do plants and quadrupeds. If our bodies were fed with pure and simple elements, and not with a stimulating and heating diet, they would afford no more pasture for cold than a leafless twig, but thrive like the trees, which find even winter genial to their expansion.

The wonderful purity of nature at this season is a most pleasing fact. Every decayed stump and moss-grown stone and rail, and the dead leaves of autumn, are concealed by a clean napkin of snow. In the bare fields and tinkling woods, see what virtue survives. In the coldest and bleakest places, the warmest charities still maintain a foothold. A cold and searching wind drives away all contagion, and nothing can withstand it but what has a virtue in it, and accordingly, whatever we meet with in cold and bleak places, as the tops of mountains, we respect for a sort of sturdy innocence, a Puritan toughness. All things beside seem to be called in for shelter, and what stays out must be part of the original frame of the universe, and of such valor as God himself. It is invigorating to breathe the cleansed air. Its greater fineness and purity are visible to the eye, and we would fain stay out long and late, that the gales may sigh through us, too, as through the leafless trees, and fit us for the winter, as if we hoped so to borrow some pure and steadfast virtue, which will stead us in all seasons.

There is a slumbering subterranean fire in nature which never goes out, and which no cold can chill. It finally melts the great snow, and in January or July is only buried under a thicker or thinner covering. In the coldest day it flows somewhere, and the snow melts around every tree. This field of winter rye, which sprouted late in the fall, and now speedily dissolves the snow, is where the fire is very thinly covered. We feel warmed by it. In the winter, warmth stands for all virtue, and we resort in thought to a trickling rill, with its bare stones shining in the sun, and to warm springs in the woods, with as much eagerness as rabbits and robins. The steam which rises from swamps and pools is as dear and domestic as that of our own kettle. What fire could ever equal the sunshine of a winter's day, when the meadow mice come out by the wall-sides, and the chickadee lisps in the defiles of the wood? The warmth comes directly from the sun, and is not radiated from the earth, as in summer; and when we feel his beams on our backs as we are treading some snowy dell, we are grateful as for a special kindness, and bless the sun which has followed us into that by-place.

This subterranean fire has its altar in each man's breast; for in the coldest day, and on the bleakest hill, the traveler cherishes a warmer fire within the folds of his cloak than is kindled on any hearth. A healthy man, indeed, is the complement of the seasons, and in winter, summer is in his heart. There is the south.

Thither have all birds and insects migrated, and around the warm springs in his breast are gathered the robin and the lark.

At length, having reached the edge of the woods, and shut out the gadding town, we enter within their covert as we go under the roof of a cottage, and cross its threshold, all ceiled and banked up with snow. They are glad and warm still, and as genial and cheery in winter as in summer. As we stand in the midst of the pines in the flickering and checkered light which straggles but little way into their maze, we wonder if the towns have ever heard their simple story. It seems to us that no traveler has ever explored them, and notwithstanding the wonders which science is elsewhere revealing every day, who would not like to hear their annals? Our humble villages in the plain are their contribution. We borrow from the forest the boards which shelter and the sticks which warm us.

How important is their evergreen to the winter, that portion of the summer which does not fade, the permanent year, the unwithered grass! Thus simply, and with little expense of altitude, is the surface of the earth diversified. What would human life be without forests, those natural cities? From the tops of mountains they appear like smooth-shaven lawns, yet whither shall we walk but in this taller grass?

In this glade covered with bushes of a year's growth, see how the silvery dust lies on every seared leaf and twig, deposited in such infinite and luxurious forms as by their very variety atone for the absence of color. Observe the tiny tracks of mice around every stem, and the triangular tracks of the rabbit. A pure elastic heaven hangs over all, as if the impurities of the summer sky, refined and shrunk by the chaste winter's cold, had been winnowed from the heavens upon the earth.

Nature confounds her summer distinctions at this season. The heavens seem to be nearer the earth. The elements are less reserved and distinct. Water turns to ice, rain to snow. The day is but a Scandinavian night. The winter is an arctic summer.

How much more living is the life that is in nature, the furred life which still survives the stinging nights, and, from amidst fields and woods covered with frost and snow, sees the sun rise:

> The foodless wilds
> Pour forth their brown inhabitants.

The gray squirrel and rabbit are brisk and playful in the remote glens, even on the morning of the cold Friday. Here is our Lapland and Labrador, and for our Esquimaux and Knistenaux, Dog-ribbed Indians, Novazemblaites, and Spitzbergeners, are there not the ice-cutter and woodchopper, the fox, muskrat, and mink?

As the day advances, the heat of the sun is

reflected by the hillsides, and we hear a faint but sweet music, where flows the rill released from its fetters, and the icicles are melting on the trees; and the nuthatch and partridge are heard and seen. The south wind melts the snow at noon, and the bare ground appears with its withered grass and leaves, and we are invigorated by the perfume which exhales from it, as by the scent of strong meats.

Now our path begins to ascend gradually to the top of this high hill, from whose precipitous south side we can look over the broad country of forest and field and river, to the distant snowy mountains. See yonder thin column of smoke curling up through the woods from some invisible farmhouse, the standard raised over some rural homestead. There must be a warmer and more genial spot there below, as where we detect the vapor from a spring forming a cloud above the trees. What fine relations are established between the traveler who discovers this airy column from some eminence in the forest and him who sits below! Up goes the smoke as silently and naturally as the vapor exhales from the leaves, and as busy disposing itself in wreaths as the housewife on the hearth below. It is a hieroglyphic of man's life, and suggests more intimate and important things than the boiling of a pot. Where its fine column rises above the forest, like an ensign, some human life has planted itself, and such is the beginning of Rome, the establishment of the arts, and the foundation of empires, whether on the prairies of America or the steppes of Asia.

And now we descend again, to the brink of this woodland lake, which lies in a hollow of the hills, as if it were their expressed juice, and that of the leaves which are annually steeped in it. Without outlet or inlet to the eye, it has still its history, in the lapse of its waves, in the rounded pebbles on its shore, and in the pines which grow down to its brink. It has not been idle, though sedentary, but, like Abu Musa, teaches that 'sitting still at home is the heavenly way; the going out is the way of the world'. Yet in its evaporation it travels as far as any. In summer it is the earth's liquid eye, a mirror in the breast of nature. The sins of the wood are washed out in it. See how the woods form an amphitheatre about it, and it is an arena for all the genialness of nature. All trees direct the traveller to its brink, all paths seek it out, birds fly to it, quadrupeds flee to it, and the very ground inclines toward it. It is nature's saloon, where she has sat down to her toilet. Consider her silent economy and tidiness; how the sun comes with his evaporation to sweep the dust from its surface each morning, and a fresh surface is constantly welling up; and annually, after whatever impurities have accumulated herein, its liquid transparency appears again in the spring. In summer a hushed music seems to sweep across its surface. But now a plain sheet of snow conceals it from our eyes, except where the wind has swept the ice bare, and the sere leaves are gliding from side to side, tacking and veering on their tiny voyages. Here is one just keeled up against a pebble on shore, a dry beech leaf, rocking still, as if it would start again. A skilful engineer, methinks, might project its course since it fell from the parent stem. Here are all the elements for such a calculation. Its present position, the direction of the wind, the level of the pond, and how much more is given. In its scarred edges and veins is its log rolled up.

We fancy ourselves in the interior of a larger house. The surface of the pond is our deal table or sanded floor, and the woods rise abruptly from its edge, like the walls of a cottage. The lines set to catch pickerel through the ice look like a larger culinary preparation, and the men stand about on the white ground like pieces of forest furniture. The actions of these men, at the distance of half a mile over the ice and snow, impress us as when we read the exploits of Alexander in history. They seem not unworthy of the scenery, and as momentous as the conquest of kingdoms.

Again we have wandered through the arches of the wood, until from its skirts we hear the distant booming of ice from yonder bay of the river, as if it were moved by some other and subtler tide than oceans know. To me it has a strange sound of home, thrilling as the voice of one's distant and noble kindred. A mild summer sun shines over forest and lake, and though there is but one green leaf for many rods, yet nature enjoys a serene health. Every sound is fraught with the same mysterious assurance of health, as well now the creaking of the boughs in January, as the soft sough of the wind in July.

In winter, nature is a cabinet of curiosities, full of dried specimens, in their natural order and position. The meadows and forests are a *hortus siccus*. The leaves and grasses stand perfectly pressed by the air without screw or gum, and the birds' nests are not hung on an artificial twig, but where they builded them. We go about dry-shod to inspect the summer's work in the rank swamp, and see what a growth have got the alders, the willows, and the maples; testifying to how many warm suns, and fertilizing dews and showers. See what strides their boughs took in the luxuriant summer, and anon these dormant buds will carry them onward and upward another span into the heavens.

Occasionally we wade through fields of snow, under whose depths the river is lost for many rods, to appear again to the right or left, where we least expected; still holding on its way underneath, with a faint, stertorous, rumbling sound, as if, like the bear and marmot, it too had hibernated, and we had followed its faint summer trail to where it earthed itself in snow and ice. At first we should have thought that rivers would be empty and dry in midwinter, or else frozen solid till the spring thawed them; but their volume is not diminished even, for only a superficial cold bridges their surfaces. The thousand springs which feed the lakes and streams are flowing still. The issues of a few surface springs only are closed, and they go to swell the deep reservoirs. Nature's wells are below the frost. The summer brooks are not filled with snow-water, nor does the mower quench his thirst with that alone. The streams are swollen when the snow melts in the spring, because nature's work has been delayed, the water being turned into ice and snow, whose particles are less smooth and round, and do not find their level so soon.

Far over the ice, between the hemlock woods and snow-clad hills, stands the pickerel-fisher, his lines set in some retired cove, like a Finlander, with his arms thrust into the pouches of his dreadnaught; with dull, snowy, fishy thoughts, himself a finless fish, separated a few inches from his race; dumb, erect, and made to be enveloped in clouds and snows, like the pines on shore. In these wild scenes, men stand about in the scenery, or move deliberately and heavily, having sacrificed the sprightliness and vivacity of towns to the dumb sobriety of nature. He does not make the scenery less wild, more than the jays and muskrats, but stands there as a part of it, as the natives are represented in the voyages of early navigators, at Nootka Sound, and on the Northwest coast, with their furs about them, before they were tempted to loquacity by a scrap of iron. He belongs to the natural family of man, and is planted deeper in nature and has more root than the inhabitants of towns. Go to him, ask what luck, and you will learn that he too is a worshiper of the unseen. Hear with what sincere deference and waving gesture in his tone he speaks of the lake pickerel, which he has never seen, his primitive and ideal race of pickerel. He is connected with the shore still, as by a fish-line, and yet remembers the season when he took fish through the ice on the pond, while the peas were up in his garden at home.

But now, while we have loitered, the clouds have gathered again, and a few straggling snowflakes are beginning to descend. Faster and faster they fall, shutting out the distant objects from sight. The snow falls on every wood and field, and no crevice is forgotten; by the river and the pond, on the hill and in the valley. Quadrupeds are confined to their coverts and the birds sit upon their perches this peaceful hour. There is not so much sound as in fair weather, but silently and gradually every slope, and the gray walls and fences, and the polished ice, and the sere leaves, which were not buried before, are concealed, and the tracks of men and beasts are lost. With so little effort does nature reassert her rule and blot out the traces of men. Hear how Homer has described the same: 'The snowflakes fall thick and fast on a winter's day. The winds are lulled, and the snow falls incessant, covering the tops of the mountains, and the hills, and the plains where the lotus-tree grows, and the cultivated fields, and they are falling by the inlets and shores of the foaming sea, but are silently dissolved by the waves.' The snow levels all things, and infolds them deeper in the bosom of nature, as, in the slow summer, vegetation creeps up to the entablature of the temple, and the turrets of the castle, and helps her to prevail over art.

The surly night-wind rustles through the wood, and warns us to retrace our steps, while the sun goes down behind the thickening storm, and birds seek their roosts, and cattle their stalls.

> Drooping the lab'rer ox
> Stands covered o'er with snow, and now demands
> The fruit of all his toil.

Though winter is represented in the almanac as an old man, facing the wind and sleet, and drawing his cloak about him, we rather think of him as a merry woodchopper, and warm-blooded youth, as blithe as summer. The unexplored grandeur of the storm keeps up the spirits of the traveler. It does not trifle with us, but has a sweet earnestness. In winter we lead a more inward life. Our hearts are warm and cheery, like cottages under drifts, whose windows and doors are half concealed, but from whose chimneys the smoke cheerfully ascends. The imprisoning drifts increase the sense of comfort which the house affords, and in the coldest days we are content to sit over the hearth and see the sky through the chimney-top, enjoying the quiet and serene life that may be had in a warm corner by the chimney-side, or feeling our pulse by listening to the low of cattle in the street, or the sound of the flail in distant barns all the long afternoon. No doubt a skilful physician could determine our health by observing how these simple and natural sounds affected us. We enjoy now, not an Oriental, but a Boreal leisure, around warm stoves and fireplaces, and watch the shadow of motes in the sunbeams.

Sometimes our fate grows too homely and familiarly serious ever to be cruel. Consider how for three months the human destiny is wrapped in furs. The good Hebrew Revelation takes no cognizance of all this cheerful snow. Is there no religion for the temperate and frigid zones? We know of no scripture which records the pure benignity of the gods on a New England winter night. Their praises have never been sung, only their wrath deprecated. The best scripture, after all, records but a meagre faith. Its saints live reserved and austere. Let a brave, devout man spend the year in the woods of Maine or Labrador, and see if the Hebrew Scriptures speak adequately to his condition and experience, from the setting in of winter to the breaking up of the ice.

Now commences the long winter evening around the farmer's hearth, when the thoughts of the indwellers travel far abroad, and men are by nature and necessity charitable and liberal to all creatures. Now is the happy resistance to cold, when the farmer reaps his reward, and thinks of his preparedness for winter, and, through the glittering panes, sees with equanimity 'the mansion of the northern bear' for now the storm is over.

> The full ethereal round,
> Infinite worlds disclosing to the view,
> Shines out intensely keen; and all one cope
> Of starry glitter glows from pole to pole.

From 'A Winter Walk', 1843

N. Brooke, MD

– Never Look Up –

I encountered Mr Hackman, an Englishman, who has been walking the length and breadth of Europe for several years. I enquired of him what were his chief observations. He replied gruffly: 'I never look up,' and went on his way.

N. Brooke, MD, 1796

Mark Twain

– The Fog Shut Down on Us –

T he Rigi-Kulm is an imposing Alpine mass, six thousand feet high, which stands by itself, and commands a mighty prospect of blue lakes, green valleys, and snowy mountains a compact and magnificent picture three hundred miles in circumference. The ascent is made by rail, or horseback, or on foot, as one may prefer. I and my agent panoplied ourselves in walking-costume, one bright morning, and started down the lake on the steamboat; we got ashore at the village of Waeggis; three-quarters of an hour distant from Lucerne. This village is at the foot of the mountain.

We were soon tramping leisurely up the leafy mule-path, and then the talk began to flow, as usual. It was twelve o'clock noon, and a breezy, cloudless day; the ascent was gradual, and the glimpses, from under the curtaining boughs, of blue water, and tiny sailboats, and beetling cliffs, were as charming as glimpses of dreamland. All the circumstances were perfect – and the anticipations, too, for we should soon be enjoying, for the first time, that wonderful spectacle, an Alpine sunrise – the object of our journey. There was (apparently) no real need for hurry, for the guidebook made the walking-distance from Waeggis to the summit only three hours and a quarter. I say 'apparently', because the guidebook had already fooled us once – about the distance from Allerheiligen to Oppenau – and for aught I knew it might be getting ready to fool us again. We were only certain as to the altitudes – we calculated to find out for ourselves how many hours it is from the bottom to the top. The summit is six thousand feet above the sea, but only forty-five hundred feet above the lake. When we had walked half an hour, we were fairly into the swing and humor of the undertaking, so we cleared for action; that is to say, we got a boy whom we met to carry our alpenstocks and satchels and overcoats and things for us; that left us free for business. I suppose we must have stopped oftener to stretch out on the grass in the shade and take a bit of a smoke than this boy was used to, for presently he asked if it had been our idea to hire him by the job, or by the year? We told him he could move along if he was in a hurry. He said he wasn't in such a very particular hurry, but he wanted to get to the top while he was young.

We told him to clear out, then, and leave the things at the uppermost hotel and say we should be along presently. He said he would secure us a hotel if he could, but if they were all full he would ask them to build another one and hurry up and get the paint and plaster dry against we arrived. Still gently chaffing us, he pushed ahead, up the trail, and soon disappeared. By six o'clock we were pretty high up in the air, and the view of lake and mountains had greatly grown in breadth and interest. We halted awhile at a little public house, where we had bread and cheese and a quart or two of fresh milk, out on the porch, with the big panorama all before us – and then moved on again.

Ten minutes afterward we met a hot, red-face man plunging down the mountain, making mighty strides, swinging his alpenstock ahead of him, and taking a grip on the ground with its iron point to support these big strides. He stopped, fanned himself with his hat, swabbed the perspiration from his face and neck with a red handkerchief, panted a moment or two, and asked how far to Waeggis. I said three hours

He looked surprised, and said: 'Why, it seems as if I could toss a biscuit into the lake from here, it's so close by. Is that an inn, there?'

I said it was.

'Well,' said he, 'I can't stand another three hours, I've had enough today; I'll take a bed there.'

I asked: 'Are we nearly to the top?'

'Nearly to the *top*? Why, bless your soul, you haven't really started, yet.'

I said we would put up at the inn, too. So we turned back and ordered a hot supper, and had quite a jolly evening of it with this Englishman.

The German landlady gave us neat rooms and

nice beds, and when I and my agent turned in, it was with the resolution to be up early and make the utmost of our first Alpine sunrise. But of course we were dead tired, and slept like policemen; so when we awoke in the morning and ran to the window it was already too late, because it was half past eleven. It was a sharp disappointment. However, we ordered breakfast and told the landlady to call the Englishman, but she said he was already up and off at daybreak – and swearing like mad about something or other. We could not find out what the matter was. He had asked the landlady the altitude of her place above the level of the lake, and she told him fourteen hundred and ninety-five feet. That was all that was said; then he lost his temper. He said that between fools and guidebooks, a man could acquire ignorance enough in twenty-four hours in a country like this to last him a year. Harris believed our boy had been loading him up with misinformation; and this was probably the case, for his epithet described that boy to a dot.

We got under way about the turn of noon, and pulled out for the summit again, with a fresh and vigorous step. When we had gone about two hundred yards, and stopped to rest, I glanced to the left while I was lighting my pipe, and in the distance detected a long worm of black smoke crawling lazily up the steep mountain. Of course that was the locomotive. We propped ourselves on our elbows at once, to gaze, for we had never seen a mountain railway yet. Presently we could make out the train. It seemed incredible that that thing should creep straight up a sharp slant like the roof of a house – but there it was, and it was doing that very miracle.

In the course of a couple hours we reached a fine breezy altitude where the little shepherd huts had big stones all over their roofs to hold them down to the earth when the great storms rage. The country was wild and rocky about here, but there were plenty of trees, plenty of moss, and grass.

Away off on the opposite shore of the lake we could see some villages, and now for the first time we could observe the real difference between their proportions and those of the giant mountains at whose feet they slept. When one is in one of those villages it seems spacious, and its houses seem high and not out of proportion to the mountain that overhangs them – but from our altitude, what a change! The mountains were bigger and grander than ever, as they stood there thinking their solemn thoughts with their heads in the drifting clouds, but the villages at their feet – when the painstaking eye could trace them up and find them – were so reduced, almost invisible, and lay so flat against the ground, that the exactest simile I can devise is to compare them to ant-deposits of granulated dirt overshadowed by the huge bulk of a cathedral. The steamboats skimming along under the stupendous precipices were diminished by distance to the daintiest little toys, the sailboats and rowboats to shallops proper for fairies that keep house in the cups of lilies and ride to court on the backs of bumblebees.

Presently we came upon half a dozen sheep nibbling grass in the spray of a stream of clear water that sprang from a rock wall a hundred feet high, and all at once our ears were startled with a melodious 'Lul ... l ... l l l llul-lul-LAhee-o-o-o!' pealing joyously from a near but invisible source, and recognized that we were hearing for the first time the famous Alpine *Jodel* in its own native wilds. And we recognized, also, that it was that sort of quaint commingling of baritone and falsetto which at home we call 'Tyrolese warbling.'

The jodeling (pronounced yOdling – emphasis on the O) continued, and was very pleasant and inspiriting to hear. Now the jodeler appeared – a shepherd boy of sixteen – and in our gladness and gratitude we gave him a franc to jodel some more. So he jodeled and we listened. We moved on, presently, and he generously jodeled us out of sight. After about fifteen minutes we came across another shepherd boy who was jodeling, and gave him half a franc to keep it up. He also jodeled us out of sight. After that, we found a jodeler every ten minutes; we gave the first one eight cents, the second one six cents, the third one four, the fourth one a penny, contributed nothing to Nos. 5, 6, and 7, and during the remainder of the day hired the rest of the jodelers, at a franc apiece, not to jodel any more. There is somewhat too much of the jodeling in the Alps.

About the middle of the afternoon we passed through a prodigious natural gateway called the Felsenthor, formed by two enormous upright rocks, with a third lying across the top. There was a very attractive little hotel close by, but our energies were not conquered yet, so we went on.

Three hours afterward we came to the railway-track. It was planted straight up the mountain with the slant of a ladder that leans against a house, and it seemed to us that man would need good nerves who proposed to travel up it or down it either.

During the latter part of the afternoon we cooled our roasting interiors with ice-cold water from clear streams, the only really satisfying water we had tasted since we left home, for at the hotels on the continent they merely give you a tumbler of ice to soak your water in, and that only modifies its hotness, doesn't make it cold. Water can only be made cold enough for summer comfort by being prepared in a refrigerator or a closed ice-pitcher. Europeans say ice-water impairs digestion. How do they know? – they never drink any.

At ten minutes past six we reached the Kaltbad station, where there is a spacious hotel with great verandas which command a majestic expanse of lake and mountain scenery. We were pretty well fagged out, now, but as we did not wish to miss the Alpine sunrise, we got through our dinner as quickly as possible and hurried off to bed. It was unspeakably comfortable to stretch our weary limbs between the cool, damp sheets. And how we did sleep! – for there is no opiate like Alpine pedestrianism.

In the morning we both awoke and leaped out of bed at the same instant and ran and stripped aside the window-curtains; but we suffered a bitter disappointment again: it was already half past three in the afternoon.

We dressed sullenly and in ill spirits, each accusing the other of oversleeping. Harris said if we had brought the courier along, as we ought to have done, we should not have missed these sunrises. I said he knew very well that one of us would have to sit up and wake the courier; and I added that we were having trouble enough to take care of ourselves, on this climb, without having to take care of a courier besides.

During breakfast our spirits came up a little, since we found by this guidebook that in the hotels on the summit the tourist is not left to trust to luck for his sunrise, but is roused betimes by a man who goes through the halls with a great Alpine horn, blowing blasts that would raise the dead. And there was another consoling thing: the guidebook said that up there on the summit the guests did not wait to dress much, but seized a red bed blanket and sailed out arrayed like an Indian. This was good; this would be romantic; two hundred and fifty people grouped on the windy summit, with their hair flying and their red blankets flapping, in the solemn presence of the coming sun, would be a striking and memorable spectacle. So it was good luck, not ill luck, that we had missed those other sunrises.

We were informed by the guidebook that we were now 3,228 feet above the level of the lake – therefore full two-thirds of our journey had been accomplished. We got away at a quarter past four p.m.; a hundred yards above the hotel the railway divided; one track went straight up the steep hill, the other one turned square off to the right, with a very slight grade. We took the latter, and followed it more than a mile, turned a rocky corner, and came in sight of a handsome new hotel. If we had gone on, we should have arrived at the summit, but Harris preferred to ask a lot of questions – as usual, of a man who didn't know anything – and he told us to go back and follow the other route. We did so. We could ill afford this loss of time.

We climbed and climbed; and we kept on climbing; we reached about forty summits, but there was always another one just ahead. It came on to rain, and it rained in dead earnest. We were soaked through and it was bitter cold. Next a smoky fog of clouds covered the whole region densely, and we took to the railway-ties to keep from getting lost. Sometimes we slopped along in a narrow path on the left-hand side of the track, but by and by when the fog blew aside a little and we saw that we were treading the rampart of a precipice and that our left elbows were projecting over a perfectly boundless and bottomless vacancy, we gasped, and jumped for the ties again.

The night shut down, dark and drizzly and cold. About eight in the evening the fog lifted and showed us a well-worn path which led up a very steep rise to the left. We took it, and as soon as we had got far enough from the railway to render the finding it again an impossibility, the fog shut down on us once more.

We were in a bleak, unsheltered place, now, and had to trudge right along, in order to keep warm, though we rather expected to go over a precipice, sooner or later. About nine o'clock we made an important discovery – that we were not in any path. We groped around a while on our hands and knees, but we could not find it; so we sat down in the mud and the wet scant grass to wait.

We were terrified into this by being suddenly confronted with a vast body which showed itself vaguely for an instant and in the next instant was smothered in the fog again. It was really the hotel we were after, monstrously magnified by the fog, but we took it for the face of a precipice, and decided not to try to claw up it.

We sat there an hour, with chattering teeth and quivering bodies, and quarrelled over all sorts of trifles, but gave most of our attention to abusing each other for the stupidity of deserting the railway-track. We sat with our backs to the precipice, because what little wind there was came from that quarter. At some time or other the fog thinned a little; we did not know when, for we were facing the empty universe and the thinness could not show; but at last Harris happened to look around, and there stood a huge, dim, spectral hotel where the precipice had been. One could faintly discern the windows and chimneys, and a dull blur of lights. Our first emotion was deep, unutterable gratitude, our next was a foolish rage, born of the suspicion that possibly the hotel had been visible three-quarters of an hour while we sat there in those cold puddles quarrelling.

Yes, it was the Rigi-Kulm hotel – the one that occupies the extreme summit, and whose remote little sparkle of lights we had often seen glinting high aloft among the stars from our balcony away down yonder in Lucerne. The crusty portier and the crusty clerks gave us the surly reception which their kind deal out in prosperous times, but by mollifying them with an extra display of obsequiousness and servility we finally got them to show us to the room which our boy had engaged for us.

We got into some dry clothing, and while our supper was preparing we loafed forsakenly through a couple of vast cavernous drawing-rooms, one of which had a stove in it. This stove was in a corner, and densely walled around with people. We could not get near the fire, so we moved at large in the artic spaces, among a multitude of people who sat silent, smileless, forlorn, and shivering – thinking what fools they were to come, perhaps. There were some Americans and some Germans, but one could see that the great majority were English.

We lounged into an apartment where there was a great crowd, to see what was going on. It was a memento-magazine. The tourists were eagerly buying all sorts and styles of paper-cutters, marked 'Souvenir of the Rigi', with handles made of the little curved horn of the ostensible chamois; there were all manner of wooden goblets and such things, similarly marked. I was going to buy a paper-cutter, but I believed I could remember the cold comfort of the Rigi-Kulm without it, so I smothered the impulse.

Supper warmed us, and we went immediately to bed – but first, as Mr Baedeker requests all tourists to call his attention to any errors which they may find in his guidebooks, I dropped him a line to inform him he missed it by just about three days. I had previously informed him of his mistake about the distance from Allerheiligen to Oppenau, and had also informed the Ordnance Depart of the German government of the same error in the imperial maps. I will add, here, that I never got any answer to those letters, or any thanks from either of those sources; and, what is still more discourteous, these corrections have not been made, either in the maps or the guidebooks. But I will write again when I get time, for my letters may have miscarried.

We curled up in the clammy beds, and went to sleep without rocking. We were so sodden with fatigue that we never stirred nor turned over till the blooming blasts of the Alpine horn aroused us.

It may well be imagined that we did not lose any time. We snatched on a few odds and ends of clothing, cocooned ourselves in the proper red blankets, and plunged along the halls and out into the whistling wind bareheaded. We saw a tall wooden scaffolding on the very peak of the summit, a hundred yards away, and made for it. We rushed up the stairs to the top of this scaffolding, and stood there, above the vast outlying world, with hair flying and ruddy blankets waving and cracking in the fierce breeze.

'Fifteen minutes too late, at last!' said Harris, in a vexed voice. 'The sun is clear above the horizon.'

'No matter,' I said, 'it is a most magnificent spectacle, and we will see it do the rest of its rising anyway.'

In a moment we were deeply absorbed in the

marvel before us, and dead to everything else. The great cloud-barred disk of the sun stood just above a limitless expanse of tossing white-caps – so to speak – a billowy chaos of massy mountain domes and peaks draped in imperishable snow, and flooded with an opaline glory of changing and dissolving splendors, while through rifts in a black cloud-bank above the sun, radiating lances of diamond dust shot to the zenith. The cloven valleys of the lower world swam in a tinted mist which veiled the ruggedness of their crags and ribs and ragged forests, and turned all the forbidding region into a soft and rich and sensuous paradise.

We could not speak. We could hardly breathe. We could only gaze in drunken ecstasy and drink in it. Presently Harris exclaimed:

'Why – nation, it's going *down*!'

Perfectly true. We had missed the *morning* hornblow, and slept all day. This was stupefying.

Harris said: 'Look here, the sun isn't the spectacle – it's *us* – stacked up here on top of this gallows, in these idiotic blankets, and two hundred and fifty well-dressed men and women down here gawking up at us and not caring a straw whether the sun rises or sets, as long as they've got such a ridiculous spectacle as this to set down in their memorandum-books. They seem to be laughing their ribs loose, and there's one girl there that appears to be going all to pieces. I never saw such a man as you before.

I think you are the very last possibility in the way of an ass.'

'What have *I* done?' I answered, with heat.

'What have you done? You've got up at half past seven o'clock in the evening to see the sun rise, that's what you've done.'

'And have you done any better, I'd like to know? I've always used to get up with the lark, till I came under the petrifying influence of your turgid intellect.'

'*You* used to get up with the lark – Oh, no doubt – you'll get up with the hangman one of these days. But you ought to be ashamed to be jawing here like this, in a red blanket, on a forty-foot scaffold on top of the Alps. And no end of people down here to boot; this isn't any place for an exhibition of temper.'

And so the customary quarrel went on. When the sun was fairly down, we slipped back to the hotel in the charitable gloaming, and went to bed again. We had encountered the horn-blower on the way, and he had tried to collect compensation, not only for announcing the sunset, which we did see, but for the sunrise, which we had totally missed; but we said no, we only took our solar rations on the 'European plan' – pay for what you get. He promised to make us hear his horn in the morning, if we were alive.

From *The Rigi Kulm*, 1880

Apsley Cherry-Garrard

– Madness –

I am told that when confronted by a lunatic or one who under the influence of some great grief or shock contemplates suicide, you should take the man out-of-doors and walk him about: Nature will do the rest

From *The Worst Journey in the World,* 1922

William Hazlitt

– I Like to Go by Myself –

O ne of the pleasantest things in the world is going a journey; but I like to go by myself. I can enjoy society in a room; but out of doors, nature is company enough for me. I am then never less alone than when alone.

The fields his study, nature was his book.

I cannot see the wit of walking and talking at the same time. When I am in the country, I wish to vegetate like the country. I am not for criticizing hedgerows and black cattle. I go out of town in order to forget the town and all that is in it. There are those who for this purpose go to watering-places and carry the metropolis with them. I like more elbow-room and fewer incumbrances. I like solitude, when I give myself up to it, for the sake of solitude; nor do I ask for

– a friend in my retreat,
Whom I may whisper, solitude is sweet.

The soul of a journey is liberty, perfect liberty, to think, feel, do, just as one pleases. We go a journey chiefly to be free of all impediments and of all inconveniences; to leave ourselves behind, much more to get rid of others. It is because I want a little breathing-space to muse on indifferent matters, where Contemplation

> May plume her feathers and let grow her wings,
> That in the various bustle of resort
> Were all too ruffled, and sometimes impair'd

that I absent myself from the town for a while, without feeling at a loss the moment I am left by myself. Instead of a friend in a post-chaise or in a Tilbury, to exchange good things with and vary the same stale topics over again, for once let me have a truce with impertinence. Give me the clear blue sky over my head, and the green turf beneath my feet, a winding road before me, and a three hours' march to dinner – and then to thinking! It is hard if I cannot start some game on these lone heaths. I laugh, I run, I leap, I sing for joy. From the point of yonder rolling cloud, I plunge into my past being and revel there, as the sunburnt Indian plunges headlong into the wave that wafts him to his native shore. Then long-forgotten things, like 'sunken wrack and sumless treasures,' burst upon my eager sight, and I begin to feel, think, and be myself again. Instead of an awkward silence, broken by attempts at wit or dull commonplaces, mine is that undisturbed silence of the heart which alone is perfect eloquence. No one likes puns, alliterations, antitheses, argument, and analysis better than I do; but I sometimes had rather be without them. 'Leave, oh leave me to my repose!'

I have just now other business in hand, which would seem idle to you, but is with me 'very stuff of the conscience'. Is not this wild rose sweet without a comment? Does not this daisy leap to my heart set in its coat of emerald? Yet if I were to explain to you the circumstance that has so endeared it to me, you would only smile. Had I not better then keep it to myself, and let it serve me to brood over, from here to yonder craggy point, and from thence onward to the far-distant horizon? I should be but bad company all that way, and therefore prefer being alone. I have heard it said that you may, when the moody fit comes on, walk or ride on by yourself and indulge your reveries. But this looks like a breach of manners, a neglect of others, and you are thinking all the time that you ought to rejoin your party. 'Out upon such half-faced fellowship,' say I. I like to be either entirely to myself, or entirely at the disposal of others; to talk or be silent, to walk or sit still, to be sociable or solitary. I was pleased with an observation of Mr Cobbett's, that 'he thought it a bad French custom to drink our wine with our meals, and that an Englishman ought to do only one thing at a time.' So I cannot talk and think, or indulge in melancholy musing and lively conversation by fits and starts.

'Let me have a companion of my way,' says Sterne, 'were it but to remark how the shadows lengthen as the sun declines.' It is beautifully said; but in my opinion, this continual comparing of notes interferes with the involuntary impression of things upon the mind and hurts the sentiment. If you only hint what you feel in a kind of dumb show, it is insipid; if you have to explain it, it is making a toil of a pleasure. You cannot read the book of nature without being perpetually put to the trouble of translating it for the benefit of others. I am for the synthetical method on a journey, in preference to the analytical. I am content to lay in a stock of ideas then, and to examine and anatomize them afterwards. I want to see my vague notions float like the down of the thistle before the breeze, and not to have them entangled in the briars and thorns of controversy. For once, I like to have it all my own way; and this is impossible unless you are alone, or in such company as I do not covet. I have no objection to argue a point with any one for twenty miles of measured road, but not for pleasure. If you remark the scent of a bean-field crossing the road, perhaps your fellow-traveller has no smell. If you point to a distant object, perhaps he is shortsighted, and has to take out his glass to look at it. There is a feeling in the air, a tone in the colour of a cloud which hits your fancy, but the effect of which you are unable to account for. There is then no sympathy, but an uneasy craving after it, and a dissatisfaction which pursues you on the way, and in the end probably produces ill humour. Now I never quarrel with myself, and take all my own conclusions for granted till I find it necessary to defend them against objections. It is not merely that you may not be of accord on the objects and circumstances that present themselves before you – these may recall a number of objects and lead to associations too delicate and refined to be possibly communicated to others. Yet these I love to cherish, and sometimes still fondly clutch them, when I can escape from the throng to do so. To give way to our feelings before company, seems extravagance or affectation; and, on the other hand, to have to unravel this mystery of our being at every turn, and to make others take an equal interest in it (otherwise the end is not answered) is a task to which few are competent. We must 'give it an understanding, but no tongue'. My old friend Coleridge, however, could do both. He could go on in the most delightful explanatory way over hill and dale, a summer's day, and convert a landscape into a didactic poem or a Pindaric ode. 'He talked far above singing.' If I could so clothe my ideas in sounding and flowing words, I might perhaps wish to have someone with me to admire the swelling theme; or I could be more content, were it possible for me still to hear his echoing voice in the woods of All-Foxden. They had 'that fine madness in them which our first poets had'; and if they could have been caught by some rare instrument, would have breathed such strains as the following.

> – Here be woods as green
> As any, air likewise as fresh and sweet
> As when smooth Zephyrus plays on the fleet
> Face of the curled streams, with fiow'rs as many
> As the young spring gives, and as choice as any;
> Here be all new delights, cool streams and wells,
> Arbours o'ergrown with woodbines, caves and dells;
> Choose where thou wilt, whilst I sit by and sing,
> Or gather rushes, to make many a ring
> For thy long fingers; tell thee tales of love;
> How the pale Phoebe, hunting in a grove.
> First saw the boy Endymion, from whose eyes
> She took eternal fire that never dies;
> How she convey'd him softly in a sleep.
> His temples bound with poppy, to the steep
> Head of old Latmos, where she stoops each night,
> Gilding the mountains with her brother's light.
> To kiss her sweetest.
>
> 'Faithful Shepherdess'

Had I words and images at command like these, I would attempt to wake the thoughts that lie slumbering on golden ridges in the evening clouds; but at the sight of nature my fancy, poor as it is, droops and closes up its leaves, like flowers at sunset. I can make nothing out on the spot: – I must have time to collect myself.

In general, a good thing spoils out-of-door

prospects; it should be reserved for table-talk. Lamb is for this reason, I take it, the worst company in the world out of doors; because he is the best within. I grant, there is one subject on which it is pleasant to talk on a journey; and that is, what one shall have for supper when we get to our inn at night. The open air improves this sort of conversation or friendly altercation by setting a keener edge on appetite. Every mile of the road heightens the flavour of the viands we expect at the end of it. How fine it is to enter some old town, walled and turreted, just at the approach of nightfall, or to come to some straggling village, with the lights streaming through the surrounding gloom; and then after inquiring for the best entertainment that the place affords, to 'take one's ease at one's inn! These eventful moments in our lives' history are too precious, too full of solid, heartfelt happiness to be frittered and dribbled away in imperfect sympathy. I would have them all to myself, and drain them to the last drop; they will do to talk of or to write about afterwards. What a delicate speculation it is, after drinking whole goblets of tea, the cups that cheer, but not inebriate, and letting the fumes ascend into the brain, to sit considering what we shall have for supper – eggs and a rasher, a rabbit smothered in onions, or an excellent veal-cutlet! Sancho in such a situation once fixed on cow heel; and his choice, though he could not help it, is not to be disparaged. Then, in the intervals of pictured scenery and Shandean contemplation, to catch the preparation and the stir in the kitchen – *Procul, O procul este profani!* [trsl. far, far from the uninitiated]. These hours are sacred to silence and to musing, to be treasured up in the memory, and to feed the source of smiling thoughts hereafter. I would not waste them in idle talk; or if I must have the integrity of fancy broken in upon, I would rather it were by a stranger than a friend. A stranger takes his hue and character from the time and place; he is a part of the furniture and costume of an inn. If he is a Quaker, or from the West Riding of Yorkshire, so much the better. I do not even try to sympathize with him, and he breaks no squares. I associate nothing with my travelling companion but present objects and passing events. In his ignorance of me and my affairs, I in a manner forget myself. But a friend reminds one of other things, rips up old grievances, and destroys the abstraction of the scene. He comes in ungraciously between us and our imaginary character. Something is dropped in the course of conversation that gives a hint of your profession and pursuits; or from having someone with you that knows the less sublime portions of your history, it seems that other people do. You are no longer a citizen of the world: but your 'unhoused free condition is put into circumscription and confine.' The *incognito* of an inn is one of its striking privileges – 'Lord of one's self, uncumber'd with a name.' Oh! it is great to shake off the trammels of the world and of public opinion, to lose our importunate, tormenting, everlasting personal identity in the elements of nature, and become the creature of the moment, clear of all ties – to hold to the universe only by a dish of sweetbreads, and to owe nothing but the score of the evening – and no longer seeking for applause and meeting with contempt, to be known by no other title than *The Gentleman in the parlour!* One may take one's choice of all characters in this romantic state of uncertainty as to one's real pretensions, and become indefinitely respectable and negatively right-worshipful. We baffle prejudice and disappoint conjecture; and from being so to others, begin to be objects of curiosity and wonder even to ourselves. We are no more those hackneyed commonplaces that we appear in the world; an inn restores us to the level of nature and quits scores with society! I have certainly spent some enviable hours at inns – sometimes when I have been left entirely to myself and have tried to solve some metaphysical problem, as once at Witham-Common, where I found out the proof that likeness is not a case of the association of ideas; at other times, when there have been pictures in the room, as at St Neot's (I think it was), where I first met with Gribelin's engravings of the Cartoons, into which I entered at once, and at a little inn on the borders of Wales, where there happened to be hanging some of Westall's drawings, which I compared triumphantly (for a theory that I had, not for the admired artist) with the figure of a girl who had ferried me over the Severn, standing up in a boat between me and the twilight – at other times I might mention luxuriating in books, with a peculiar interest in this way, as I remember sitting up half the night to read *Paul and Virginia,* which I picked up at an inn at Bridgewater, after being drenched in the rain all day; and at the same place I got through two volumes of Madame D'Arblay's *Camilla.* It was on the 10th of April, 1798, that I sat down to a volume of the *New Eloise,* at the inn at Llangollen, over a bottle of sherry and a cold chicken. The letter I chose was that in which St Preux describes his feelings as he first caught a glimpse from the heights of the Jura of the Pays de Vaud, which I had brought with me as a *bon bouche* to crown the evening with. It was my birthday, and I had for the first time come from a place in the neighborhood to visit this delightful spot. The road to Llangollen turns off between Chirk and Wrexham; and on passing a certain point, you come all at once upon the valley, which opens like an amphitheatre, broad, barren hills rising in majestic state on either side, with 'green upland swells that echo to the bleat of flocks' below, and the river Dee babbling over its stony bed in the midst of them. The valley at this time 'glittered green with sunny showers', and a budding ash-tree dipped its tender branches in the chiding stream. How proud, how glad I was to walk along the high road that overlooks the delicious prospect, repeating the lines which I have just quoted from Mr Coleridge's poems!

But besides the prospect which opened beneath my feet, another also opened to my inward sight, a heavenly vision, on which were written, in letters large as Hope could make them, these four words, LIBERTY, GENIUS, LOVE, VIRTUE; which have since faded into the light of common day, or mock my idle gaze.

The beautiful is vanished, and returns not.

Still I would return some time or other to this enchanted spot; but I would return to it alone. What other self could I find to share that influx of thoughts, of regret and delight, the fragments of which I could hardly conjure up to myself, so much have they been broken and defaced! I could stand on some tall rock and overlook the precipice of years that separates me from what I then was. I was at that time going shortly to visit the poet whom I have above named. Where is he now? Not only I myself have changed; the world, which was then new to me, has become old and incorrigible. Yet will I turn to thee in thought, O sylvan Dee, in joy, in youth and gladness as thou then wert; and thou shalt always be to me the river of Paradise, where I will drink of the waters of life freely!

There is hardly anything that shows the

shortsightedness or capriciousness of the imagination more than travelling does. With change of place we change our ideas; nay, our opinions and feelings. We can by an effort indeed transport ourselves to old and long-forgotten scenes, and then the picture of the mind revives again; but we forget those that we have just left. It seems that we can think but of one place at a time. The canvas of the fancy is but of a certain extent, and if we paint one set of objects upon it, they immediately efface every other. We cannot enlarge our conceptions, we only shift our point of view. The landscape bares its bosom to the enraptured eye, we take our fill of it and seem as if we could form no other image of beauty or grandeur. We pass on and think no more of it; the horizon that shuts it from our sight, also blots it from our memory like a dream. In travelling through a wild, barren country, I can form no idea of a woody and cultivated one. It appears to me that all the world must be barren, like what I see of it. In the country we forget the town, and in town we despise the country. 'Beyond Hyde Park,' says Sir Fopling Flutter, 'all is a desert.' All that part of the map that we do not see before us is a blank. The world in our conceit of it is not much bigger than a nutshell. It is not one prospect expanded into another, county joined to county, kingdom to kingdom, lands to seas, making an image voluminous and vast; the mind can form no larger idea of space than the eye can take in at a single glance. The rest is a name written in a map, a calculation of arithmetic. For instance, what is the true signification of that immense mass of territory and population, known by the name of China to us? An inch of pasteboard on a wooden globe, of no more account than a China orange! Things near us are seen of the size of life: things at a distance are diminished to the size of the understanding. We measure the universe by ourselves, and even comprehend the texture of our own being only piecemeal. In this way, however, we remember an infinity of things and places. The mind is like a mechanical instrument that plays a great variety of tunes, but it must play them in succession. One idea recalls another, but it at the same time excludes all others. In trying to renew old recollections, we cannot as it were unfold the whole web of our existence; we must pick out the single threads. So in coming to a place where we have formerly lived and with which we have intimate associations, everyone must have found that the feeling grows more vivid the nearer we approach the spot, from the mere anticipation of the actual impression: we remember circumstances, feelings, persons, faces, names that we had not thought of for years; but for the time all the rest of the world is forgotten! – To return to the question I have quitted above. I have no objection to go to see ruins, aqueducts, pictures, in company with a friend or a party, but rather the contrary, for the former reason reversed. They are intelligible matters and will bear talking about. The sentiment here is not tacit, but communicable and overt. Salisbury Plain is barren of criticism, but Stonehenge will bear a discussion antiquarian, picturesque, and philosophical. In setting out on a party of pleasure, the first consideration always is where we shall go to; in taking a solitary ramble, the question is what we shall meet with by the way.

'The mind is its own place'; nor are we anxious to arrive at the end of our journey. I can myself do the honours indifferently well to works of art and curiosity. I once took a party to Oxford with no mean éclat – showed them that seat of the Muses at a distance,

The glistering spires and pinnacles adorn'd

descanted on the learned air that breathes from the grassy quadrangles and stone walls of halls and colleges – was at home in the Bodleian; and at Blenheim quite superseded the powdered Ciceroni that attended us, and that pointed in vain with his wand to commonplace beauties in matchless pictures.

As another exception to the above reasoning, I should not feel confident in venturing on a journey in a foreign country without a companion. I should want at intervals to hear the sound of my own language. There is an involuntary antipathy in the mind of an Englishman to foreign manners and notions that requires the assistance of social sympathy to carry it off. As the distance from home increases, this relief, which was at first a luxury, becomes a passion and an appetite. A person would almost feel stifled to find himself in the deserts of Arabia without friends and countrymen; there must be allowed to be something in the view of Athens or old Rome that claims the utterance of speech; and I own that the Pyramids are too mighty for any single contemplation. In such situations, so opposite to all one's ordinary train of ideas, one seems a species by one's-self, a limb torn off from society, unless one can meet with instant fellowship and support. Yet I did not feel this want or craving very pressing once, when I first set my foot on the laughing shores of France. Calais was peopled with novelty and delight. The confused, busy murmur of the place was like oil and wine poured into my ears; nor did the mariners' hymn, which was sung from the top of an old crazy vessel in the harbour, as the sun went down, send an alien sound into my soul. I only breathed the air of general humanity. I walked over 'the vine-covered hills and gay regions of France', erect and satisfied; for the image of man was not cast down and chained to the foot of arbitrary thrones; I was at no loss for language, for that of all the great schools of painting was open to me. The whole is vanished like a shade. Pictures, heroes, glory, freedom, all are fled: nothing

remains but the Bourbons and the French people!
– There is undoubtedly a sensation in travelling
into foreign parts that is to be had nowhere else;
but it is more pleasing at the time than lasting. It is
too remote from our habitual associations to be a
common topic of discourse or reference, and, like a
dream or another state of existence, does not piece
into our daily modes of life. It is an animated but
a momentary hallucination. It demands an effort
to exchange our actual for our ideal identity; and
to feel the pulse of our old transports revive very
keenly, we must 'jump' all our present comforts and
connexions. Our romantic and itinerant character is
not to be domesticated. Doctor Johnson remarked
how little foreign travel added to the facilities of
conversation in those who had been abroad. In fact,
the time we have spent there is both delightful and
in one sense instructive; but it appears to be cut out
of our substantial, downright existence, and never to
join kindly on to it. We are not the same, but another,
and perhaps more enviable individual, all the time we
are out of our own country. We are lost to ourselves,
as well as our friends. So the poet somewhat quaintly
sings, 'Out of my country and myself I go.'

Those who wish to forget painful thoughts do
well to absent themselves for a while from the ties
and objects that recall them; but we can be said only
to fulfill our destiny in the place that gave us birth.
I should on this account like well enough to spend

the whole of my life in travelling abroad, if I could anywhere borrow another life to spend afterwards at home!

'On Going on a Journey', 1822

Thomas De Quincey

– Never Took Any Companion Either –

I mmediately after the termination of his dinner party, Kant walked out for exercise. But on this occasion he never took any companion. Partly, perhaps, because he thought it right, after so much convivial and colloquial relaxation, to pursue his meditations. And partly (as I happen to know) for a very peculiar reason: that he wished to breathe exclusively through his nostrils, which he could not do if he were obliged continually to open his mouth in conversation. His reason for this was, that the atmospheric air, being thus carried round by a longer circuit, and reaching the lungs, therefore, in a state of less rawness, and at a temperature somewhat higher, would be less apt to irritate them. By a steady perseverance in this practice, which he constantly recommended to his friends, he flattered himself with a long immunity from coughs, colds, hoarseness, and every mode of defluxion. And the fact really was, that these troublesome affections attacked him very rarely.

From *The Last Days of Immanuel Kant*, 1862

Petrarch

– Choose Company with Unusual Care –

When I came to look about for a companion I found, strangely enough, that hardly one among my friends seemed suitable, so rarely do we meet with just the right combination of personal tastes and characteristics, even among those who are dearest to us. This one was too apathetic, that one over-anxious; this one too slow, that one too hasty; one was too sad, another over-cheerful; one more simple, another more sagacious, than I desired. I feared this one's taciturnity and that one's loquacity. The heavy deliberation of some repelled me as much as the lean incapacity of others. I rejected those who were likely to irritate me by a cold want of interest, as well as those who might weary me by their excessive enthusiasm. Such defects, however grave, could be borne with at home, for charity suffers all things, and friendship accepts any burden; but it is quite otherwise on a journey, where every weakness becomes much more serious. So, as I was bent upon pleasure and anxious that my enjoyment should be unalloyed, I looked about me with unusual care, balanced against one another the various characteristics of my friends, and without committing any breach of friendship I silently condemned every trait which might prove disagreeable on the way. And – would you believe it? – I finally turned homeward for aid, and proposed the ascent to my only brother, who is younger than I, and with whom you are well acquainted. He was delighted and gratified beyond measure by the thought of holding the place of a friend as well as of a brother.

At the time fixed we left the house, and by evening reached Malaucene, which lies at the foot of the mountain, to the north. Having rested there a day, we finally made the ascent this morning, with no companions except two servants; and a most difficult task it was. The mountain is a very steep and almost inaccessible mass of stony soil. But, as the poet has well said, 'Remorseless toil conquers all.' It was a long day, the air fine. We enjoyed the advantages of vigour of mind and strength and agility of body, and everything else essential to those engaged in such an undertaking.

From *The Ascent of Mount Ventoux*, 1336

Charles Dickens

– A Good Humoured Multitude –

Whenever a tramp sits down to rest by the wayside, he sits with his legs in a dry ditch; and whenever he goes to sleep (which is very often indeed), he goes to sleep on his back. Yonder, by the high road, glaring white in the bright sunshine, lies, on the dusty bit of turf under the bramble-bush that fences the coppice from the highway, the tramp of the order savage, fast asleep. He lies on the broad of his back, with his face turned up to the sky, and one of his ragged arms loosely thrown across his face. His bundle (what can be the contents of that mysterious bundle, to make it worth his while to carry it about?) is thrown down beside him, and the waking woman with him sits with her legs in the ditch, and her back to the road. She wears her bonnet rakishly perched on the front of her head, to shade her face from the sun in walking, and she ties her skirts round her in conventionally tight tramp-fashion with a sort of apron. You can seldom catch sight of her, resting thus, without seeing her in a des-pondently defiant manner doing something to her hair or her bonnet, and glancing at you between her fingers. She does not often go to sleep herself in the daytime, but will sit for any length of time beside the man. And his slumberous propensities would not seem to be referable to the fatigue of carrying the bundle, for she carries it much oftener and further than he. When they are afoot, you will mostly find him slouching on ahead, in a gruff temper, while she lags heavily behind with the burden. He is given to personally correcting her, too – which phase of his character develops itself oftenest, on benches outside alehouse doors – and she appears to become strongly attached to him for these reasons; it may usually be noticed that when the poor creature has a bruised face, she is the most affectionate. He has no occupation whatever, this order of tramp, and has no object whatever in going anywhere. He will sometimes call himself a brickmaker, or a sawyer, but only when he takes an imaginary flight. He generally represents himself, in a vague way, as looking out for a job of work; but he never did work, he never does, and he never will. It is a favourite fiction with him, however (as if he were the most industrious character on earth), that *you* never work; and as he goes past your garden and sees you looking at your flowers, you will overhear him growl with a strong sense of contrast, '*You* are a lucky hidle devil, *you* are!'

The slinking tramp is of the same hopeless order, and has the same injured conviction on him that you were born to whatever you possess, and never did anything to get it: but he is of a less audacious disposition. He will stop before your gate, and say to his female companion with an air of constitutional humility and propitiation – to edify any one who may be within hearing behind a blind or a bush – 'This is a sweet spot, ain't it? A lovely spot! And I wonder if they'd give two poor footsore travellers like me and you, a drop of fresh water out of such a pretty gen-teel crib? We'd take it wery koind on 'em, wouldn't us? Wery koind, upon my word, us would?' He has a quick sense of a dog in the vicinity, and will extend his modestly-injured propitiation to the dog chained up in your yard; remarking, as he slinks at the yard gate, 'Ah! You are a foine breed o' dog, too, and *you* ain't kep for nothink! I'd take it wery koind o' your master if he'd elp a traveller and his woife as envies no gentlefolk their good fortun, wi' a bit o' your broken wittles. He'd never know the want of it, nor more would you. Don't bark like that, at poor persons as never done you no arm; the poor is downtrodden and broke enough without that; O DON'T!' He generally heaves a prodigious sigh in moving away, and always looks up the lane and down the lane, and up the road and down the road, before going on…

Towards the end of the same walk, on the same bright summer day, at the corner of the next little town or village, you may find another kind of tramp, embodied in the persons of a most exemplary couple whose only improvidence appears to have been, that they spent the last of their little All on soap. They are a man and woman, spotless to behold – John Anderson, with the frost on his short smock-frock instead of his 'pow', attended by Mrs Anderson. John is over-ostentatious of the frost upon his raiment, and wears a curious and, you would say, an almost unnecessary demonstration of girdle of white linen wound about his waist – a girdle, snowy as Mrs Anderson's apron. This cleanliness was the expiring effort of the respectable couple, and nothing then remained to Mr Anderson but to get chalked upon his spade in snow-white copybook characters, HUNGRY! and to sit down here. Yes; one thing more remained to Mr Anderson – his character; Monarchs could not deprive him of his hard-earned character. Accordingly, as you come up with this spectacle of virtue in distress, Mrs Anderson rises, and with a decent curtsey presents for your consideration a certificate from a Doctor of Divinity, the reverend the Vicar of Upper Dodgington, who informs his Christian friends and all whom it may concern that the bearers, John Anderson and lawful wife, are persons to whom you cannot be too liberal. This benevolent pastor omitted no work of his hands to fit the good couple out, for with half an eye you can recognise his autograph on the spade.

Another class of tramp is a man, the most valuable part of whose stock-in-trade is a highly perplexed demeanour. He is got up like a countryman, and you will often come upon the poor fellow, while he is endeavouring to decipher the inscription on a milestone – quite a fruitless endeavour, for he cannot read. He asks your pardon, he truly does (he is very slow of speech, this tramp, and he looks in a bewildered way all round the prospect while he talks to you), but all of us shold do as we wold be done by, and he'll take it kind, if you'll put a power man in the right road fur to jine his eldest son as has broke his leg bad in the masoning, and is in this heere Orspit'l as is wrote down by Squire Pouncerby's own hand as wold not tell a lie fur no man. He then produces from under his dark frock (being always very slow and perplexed) a neat but worn old leathern purse, from which he takes a scrap of paper. On this scrap of paper is written, by Squire Pouncerby, of The Grove, 'Please to direct the Bearer, a poor but very worthy man, to the Sussex County Hospital, near Brighton' – a matter of some difficulty at the moment, seeing that the request comes suddenly upon you in the depths of Hertfordshire. The more you endeavour to indicate where Brighton is – when you have with the greatest difficulty remembered – the less the devoted father can be made to comprehend, and the more obtusely he stares at the prospect; whereby, being reduced to extremity, you recommend the faithful parent to begin by going to St Albans, and present him with half-a-crown. It does him good, no doubt, but scarcely helps him forward, since you find him lying drunk that same evening in the wheelwright's sawpit under the shed where the felled trees are, opposite the sign of the Three Jolly Hedgers. . . .

The young fellows who trudge along barefoot, five or six together, their boots slung over their shoulders, their shabby bundles under their arms, their sticks newly cut from some roadside wood, are not eminently prepossessing, but are much less objectionable. There is a tramp-fellowship among them. They pick one another up at resting stations, and go on in companies. They always go at a fast swing – though they generally limp too – and there is invariably one of the company who has much ado to keep up with the rest. They generally talk about horses, and any other means of locomotion than walking: or, one of the company relates some recent experiences of the road – which are always disputes and difficulties. As for example. 'So as I'm a standing at the pump in the market, blest if there don't come up a Beadle, and he ses, "Mustn't stand here," he ses. "Why not?" I ses. "No beggars allowed in this town," he ses. "Who's a beggar?" I ses. "You are," he ses. "Who ever see *me* beg? Did *you*?" I ses. "Then you're a tramp," he ses. "I'd rather be that than a Beadle," I ses.' (The company express great approval.) '"Would you?" he ses to me. "Yes, I would," I ses to him. "Well," he ses, "anyhow, get out of this town." "Why, blow your little town!" I ses, "who wants to be in it? Wot does your dirty little town mean by comin' and stickin' itself in the road to anywhere? Why don't you get a shovel and a barrer, and clear your town out o' people's way?"' (The company expressing the highest approval and laughing aloud, they all go down the hill.) . . .

Who can be familiar with any rustic highway in summer-time, without storing up knowledge of the many tramps who go from one oasis of town or village to another, to sell a stock in trade, apparently not worth a shilling when sold? Shrimps are a favourite commodity for this kind of speculation, and so are cakes of a soft and spongy character, coupled with Spanish nuts and brandy balls. The stock is carried on the head in a basket, and, between the head and the basket, are the trestles on which the stock is displayed at trading times. Fleet of foot, but a careworn class of tramp this, mostly; with a certain stiffness of neck, occasioned by much anxious balancing of baskets; and also with a long, Chinese sort of eye, which an overweighted forehead would seem to have squeezed into that form.

On the hot dusty roads near seaport towns and great rivers, behold the tramping Soldier. And if you should happen never to have asked yourself whether his uniform is suited to his work, perhaps the poor fellow's appearance as he comes distressfully towards you, with his absurdly tight jacket unbuttoned, his neck-gear in his hand, and his legs well chafed by his trousers of baize, may suggest the personal inquiry, how you think *you* would like it. Much better the tramping Sailor, although his cloth is somewhat too thick for land service. But, why the tramping merchant-mate should put on a black velvet waistcoat, for a chalky country in the dog-days, is one of the great secrets of nature that will never be discovered.

I have my eye upon a piece of Kentish road, bordered on either side by a wood, and having on one hand, between the road-dust and the trees, a skirting patch of grass. Wild flowers grow in abundance on this spot, and it lies high and airy, with a distant river stealing steadily away to the ocean, like a man's life. To gain the milestone here, which the moss, primroses, violets, blue-bells, and wild roses, would soon render illegible but for peering travellers pushing them aside with their sticks, you must come up a steep hill, come which way you may. So, all the tramps with carts or caravans – the Gipsy-tramp, the Show-tramp, the Cheap Jack – find it impossible to resist the temptations of the place, and all turn the horse loose when they come to it, and boil the pot. Bless the place, I love the ashes of the vagabond fires that have scorched its grass! What tramp children do I see here, attired in a handful of rags, making a gymnasium of the shafts of the cart, making a feather-bed of the flints and brambles, making a toy of the hobbled old horse who is not much more like a horse than any cheap toy would be! Here, do I encounter the cart of mats and brooms and baskets – with all thoughts of business given to the evening wind – with the stew made and being served out – with Cheap Jack and Dear Jill striking soft music out of the plates that are rattled like warlike cymbals when put up for auction at fairs and markets – their minds so influenced (no doubt) by the melody of the nightingales as they begin to sing in the woods behind them, that if I were to propose to deal, they would sell me anything at cost price. On this hallowed ground has it been my happy privilege (let me whisper it), to behold the White-haired Lady with the pink eyes, eating meat-pie with the Giant: while, by the hedgeside, on the box of blankets which I knew contained the snakes, were set forth the cups and saucers and the teapot. It was on an evening in August, that I chanced upon this ravishing spectacle, and I noticed that, whereas the Giant reclined half concealed beneath the overhanging boughs and seemed indifferent to Nature, the white hair of the gracious Lady streamed free in the breath of evening, and her pink eyes found pleasure in the landscape. I heard only a single sentence of her uttering, yet it bespoke a talent for modest repartee. The ill-mannered Giant – accursed be his evil race! – had interrupted the Lady in some remark, and, as I passed that enchanted corner of the wood, she gently reproved him, with the words,

'Now, Cobby;' – Cobby! so short a name! – 'ain't one fool enough to talk at a time?'

Within appropriate distance of this magic ground, though not so near it as that the song trolled from tap or bench at door, can invade its woodland silence, is a little hostelry which no man possessed of a penny was ever known to pass in warm weather. Before its entrance, are certain pleasant, trimmed limes; likewise, a cool well, with so musical a bucket-handle that its fall upon the bucket rim will make a horse prick up his ears and neigh, upon the droughty road half a mile off. This is a house of great resort for haymaking tramps and harvest tramps, insomuch that as they sit within, drinking their mugs of beer, their relinquished scythes and reaping-hooks glare out of the open windows, as if the whole establishment were a family war-coach of Ancient Britons. Later in the season, the whole countryside, for miles and miles, will swarm with hopping tramps. They come in families, men, women, and children, every family provided with a bundle of bedding, an iron pot, a number of babies, and too often with some poor sick creature quite unfit for the rough life, for whom they suppose the smell of the fresh hop to be a sovereign remedy. Many of these hoppers are Irish, but many come from London. They crowd all the roads, and camp under all the hedges and on all the scraps of common-land, and live among and upon the hops until they are all picked, and the hop-gardens, so beautiful through the summer, look as if they had been laid waste by an invading army. Then, there is a vast exodus of tramps out of the country; and if you ride or drive round any turn of any road, at more than a foot pace, you will be bewildered to find that you have charged into the bosom of fifty families, and that there are splashing up all around you, in the utmost prodigality of confusion, bundles of bedding, babies, iron pots, and a good-humoured multitude of both sexes and all ages, equally divided between perspiration and intoxication.

From 'Tramps', 1860

Jean-Jacques Rousseau

– She Wanted to Take a Walk –

We had put up outside the town at Saint Jacques. I shall always remember that inn, and the room in it which Mme de Larnage occupied. After dinner she wanted to take a walk. She knew that the Marquis was no walker, and this was her way of contriving a *tête-à-tête*, which she had decided to make good use of, for there was no time to lose if any was to be left for any enjoyment. We walked around the town by the side of the moat. There I resumed the long story of my illness, and she replied to me in so tender a tone, clasping my arm and sometimes pressing it to her heart, that only stupidity like mine could have prevented me from realising that she meant what she said. The preposterous thing was that I was extremely moved myself. I have said that she was pleasing; love made her attractive, giving her back all the sparkle of her early youth; and she made her advances so cunningly that she would have seduced even a man on his guard. I was very ill at ease therefore, and always on the point of taking some liberty; but I was restrained by the fear of offending or taking some liberty; and by the greater fear of being hissed and booed and ridiculed, of providing an after dinner anecdote and on being congratulated on my enterprise by the pitiless Marquis. I was angry with myself for my stupid bashfulness and for being unable to overcome it; but at the same time I reproached myself for it. I was in tortures. I had already abandoned my shy lover's language, of which I realised the full absurdity now that I was well on the road. But, not knowing what manner to adopt or what to say, I remained silent, and looked sulky. In fact I did everything in my power to court the treatment I had feared. Fortunately Mme de Lanarge took a more humane line. She abruptly cut this silence short by putting her arm round my neck; and in a second her lips, pressed upon my own, spoke too clearly to leave me in doubt. The crisis could not have come at a happier moment. I became charming. It was time.

From *Confessions*, 1781 (trans. J. M. Cohen, 1953)

Leslie Stephen

– Great Men Have Been Enthusiastic Walkers –

W alking is the natural recreation for a man who desires not absolutely to suppress his intellect but to turn it out to play for a season. All great men of letters have, therefore, been enthusiastic walkers (exceptions, of course, excepted).

Shakespeare, besides being a sportsman, a lawyer, a divine, and so forth, conscientiously observed his own maxim, 'Jog on, jog on, the footpath way'; though a full proof of this could only be given in an octavo volume. Anyhow, he divined the connection between walking and a 'merry heart'; that is, of course, a cheerful acceptance of our position in the universe founded upon the deepest moral and philosophical principles. His friend, Ben Jonson, walked from London to Scotland. Another gentleman of the period (I forget his name) danced from London to Norwich. Tom Coryate hung up in his parish church the shoes in which he walked from Venice and then started to walk (with occasional lifts) to India. Contemporary walkers of more serious character might be quoted, such as the admirable Barclay, the famous Quaker apologist, from whom the great Captain Barclay inherited his prowess. Every one, too, must remember the incident in Walton's *Life of Hooker*. Walking from Oxford to Exeter, Hooker went to see his godfather, Bishop Jewel, at Salisbury. The bishop said that he would lend him 'a horse which hath carried me many a mile, and, I thank God, with much ease,' and 'presently delivered into his hands a walking staff with which he professed he had travelled through many parts of Germany.' He added ten groats and munificently promised ten groats more when Hooker should restore the 'horse'. When, in later days, Hooker once rode to London, he expressed more passion than that mild divine was ever known to show upon any other occasion against a friend who had dissuaded him from 'footing it'. The hack, it seems, 'trotted when he did not', and discomposed the thoughts which had been soothed by the walking staff. His biographer must be counted, I fear, among those who do not enjoy walking without the incidental stimulus of sport. Yet the *Compleat Angler* and his friends start by a walk of twenty good miles before they take their 'morning draught'. Swift, perhaps, was the first person to show a full appreciation of the moral and physical advantages of walking. He preached constantly upon this text to Stella, and practised his own advice. It is true that his notions of a journey were somewhat limited. Ten miles a day was his regular allowance when he went from London to Holyhead, but then he spent time in lounging at wayside inns to enjoy the talk of the tramps and ostlers. The fact, though his biographers are rather scandalised, shows that he really appreciated one of the true charms of pedestrian expeditions. Wesley is generally credited with certain moral reforms, but one secret of his power is not always noticed. In his early expeditions he went on foot to save horse hire, and made the great discovery that twenty or thirty miles a day was a wholesome allowance for a healthy man. The fresh air and exercise put 'spirit into his sermons', which could not be rivalled by the ordinary parson of the period, who too often passed his leisure lounging by his fireside. Fielding points the contrast. Trulliber, embodying the clerical somnolence of the day, never gets beyond his pigsties, but the model Parson Adams steps out so vigorously that he distances the stage-coach, and disappears in the distance rapt in the congenial pleasures of walking and composing a sermon. Fielding, no doubt, shared his hero's taste, and that explains the contrast between his vigorous naturalism and the sentimentalism of Richardson, who was to be seen, as he tells us, 'stealing along from Hammersmith to Kensington with his eyes on the ground, propping his unsteady limbs with a stick'. Even the ponderous Johnson used to dissipate his early hypochondria by walking from Lichfield to Birmingham and back (thirty-two miles), and his later melancholy would have changed to a more cheerful view of life could he have kept up the practice in his beloved London streets. The literary movement at the end of the eighteenth century was obviously due in great part, if not mainly, to the renewed practice of walking. Wordsworth's poetical autobiography shows how every stage in his early mental development was connected with some walk in the Lakes. The sunrise which startled him on a walk after a night spent in dancing first set him apart as a 'dedicated spirit'. His walking tour in the Alps – then a novel performance – roused him to his first considerable poem. His chief performance is the record of an excursion on foot. He kept up the practice, and De Quincey calculates somewhere what multiple of the earth's circumference he had measured on his legs, assuming, it appears, that he averaged ten miles a day. De Quincey himself, we are told, slight and fragile as he was, was a good walker, and would run up a hill 'like a squirrel'. Opium-eating is not congenial to walking, yet even Coleridge, after beginning the habit, speaks of walking forty miles a day in Scotland, and, as we all know, the great manifesto of the new school of poetry, the Lyrical Ballads, was suggested by the famous walk with Wordsworth, when the first stanzas of the 'Ancient Mariner' were composed. A remarkable illustration of the wholesome influence might be given from the cases of Scott and Byron. Scott, in spite of his lameness, delighted in walks of twenty and thirty miles a day, and in climbing crags, trusting to the strength of his arms to remedy the stumblings of his foot. The early strolls enabled him to saturate his mind with local traditions, and the passion for walking under difficulties showed the manly nature which has endeared him to three generations. Byron's lameness was too severe to admit of walking, and therefore all the unwholesome humours which would have been walked off in a good cross-country march accumulated in his brain and caused the defects, the morbid affectation and perverse misanthropy, which half ruined the achievement of the most masculine intellect of his time.

It is needless to accumulate examples of a doctrine which will no doubt be accepted as soon as it is announced. Walking is the best of panaceas for the morbid tendencies of authors. It is, I need only observe, as good for reasoners as for poets. The name of 'peripatetic' suggests the connection. Hobbes walked steadily up and down the hills in his patron's park when he was in his venerable old age. To the same practice may be justly ascribed the utilitarian philosophy. Old Jeremy Bentham kept himself up to his work for eighty years by his regular 'post-jentacular circumgyrations'. His chief disciple, James Mill, walked incessantly and preached as he walked. John Stuart Mill imbibed at once psychology, political economy, and a love of walks from his father.

Walking was his one recreation; it saved him from becoming a mere smoke-dried pedant; and though he put forward the pretext of botanical researches, it helped him to perceive that man is something besides a mere logic machine. Mill's great rival as a spiritual guide, Carlyle, was a vigorous walker, and even in his latest years was a striking figure when performing his regular constitutionals in London. One of the vivid passages in the *Reminiscences* describes his walk with Irving from Glasgow to Drumclog. Here they sat on the 'brow of a peat hag, while far, far away to the westward, over our brown horizon, towered up white and visible at the many miles of distance a high irregular pyramid. Ailsa Craig we at once guessed, and thought of the seas and oceans over yonder.' The vision naturally led to a solemn conversation, which was an event in both lives. Neither Irving nor Carlyle himself feared any amount of walking in those days, it is added, and next day Carlyle took his longest walk, fifty-four miles. Carlyle is unsurpassable in his descriptions of scenery: from the pictures of mountains in *Sartor Resartus* to the battle-pieces in *Frederick*. Ruskin, himself a good walker, is more rhetorical but not so graphic; and it is self-evident that nothing educates an eye for the features of a landscape so well as the practice of measuring it by your own legs.

The great men, it is true, have not always acknowledged their debt to the genius, whoever he may be, who presides over pedestrian exercise. Indeed, they have inclined to ignore the true source of their impulse. Even when they speak of the beauties of nature, they would give us to understand that they might have been disembodied spirits, taking aerial flights among mountain solitudes, and independent of the physical machinery of legs and stomachs . . .

From *In Praise of Walking*, 1902

Karl Philipp Moritz

– No Friendly Reception on Foot –

Windsor, 23rd June.

I have already, my dearest friend, experienced so many inconveniences on foot that I am at some loss to determine whether I shall go on in the same manner.

A traveller on foot in this country seems to be considered as a sort of wild man or out-of-the-way being. Who is stared at, pitied, suspected, and shunned by everybody that meets him. At least this has been my case on the road from Richmond to Windsor.

My host at Richmond yesterday morning could not sufficiently express his surprise that I intended to walk as far as Oxford. And farther. He however was so kind as to send his son, a clever little boy, to show me the road leading to Windsor.

At first I walked along a pleasant footway by the side of the Thames, where close to my right lay the king's garden. On the opposite bank of the Thames was Isleworth, a spot that seemed to be distinguished by some elegant gentlemen's country-seats and gardens. Here I was obliged to ferry the river in order to get into the Oxford Road, which also leads to Windsor.

When I was on the other side of the water, I came to a house and asked a man who was standing at the door if I was on the right road to Oxford. 'Yes,' said he, 'but you want a carriage to carry you thither.' When I answered him that I intended walking it, he looked at me significantly, shook his head, and went into the house again.

I was now on the road to Oxford. A charming broad road, and I met on it carriages without number, which, however, on account of the heat, occasioned a dust that was extremely troublesome and disagreeable. The fine green hedges, which border the roads in England, contribute greatly to render them pleasant. This was the case on the road I now travelled, for when I was tired I sat down in the shade under one of these hedges and read Milton. But this relief was soon disagreeable to me, for those who rode or drove past me, stared with astonishment, and made many significant gestures as if they thought my head deranged; so singular must it have appeared to them to see a man sitting along the side of a public road and reading. I therefore found myself obliged to look out for a retired spot in some by-lane or crossroad.

When I again walked, many of the coachmen who drove by called out to me, and asked if I would ride on the outside. And when, every now and then, a farmer on horseback met me, he said, and seemingly with an air of pity for me: ''Tis warm walking, sir;' and when I passed through a village, every old woman testified her pity by an exclamation of – 'Good God!'

As far as Hounslow the way was pleasant. Afterwards I thought it not quite so good. It lay across a common, which was of a considerable extent, and bare and naked, excepting that here and there I saw sheep feeding.

I now began to be very tired, when, to my astonishment, I saw a tree in the middle of the common that stood quite solitary, and spread a shade like an arbour round it. At the bottom, round the trunk, a bench was placed, on which one may sit down. Beneath the shade of this tree I reposed myself a little, read some of Milton, and made a note in my memorandum-book that I would remember this tree, which had so charitably and hospitably received under its shade a weary traveller. This, you see, I have now done.

The short English miles are delightful for walking. You are always pleased to find, every now and then, in how short a time you have walked a mile, though, no doubt, a mile is everywhere a mile. I walk but a moderate pace, and can accomplish four English miles in an hour. It used to take me pretty nearly the same time for one German mile. Now it is a pleasing exchange to find that in two hours I can walk eight miles. And now I fancy I was about seventeen miles from London, when I came to an inn, where, for a little wine and water, I was obliged to pay sixpence. An Englishman who happened to be sitting by the side of the innkeeper found out that I was a German, and, of course, from the country of his queen, in praise of whom he was quite lavish, observing more than once that England never had had such a queen, and would not easily get such another.

It now began to grow hot. On the left hand, almost close to the high road, I met with a singularly clear rivulet. In this I bathed, and was much refreshed, and afterwards, with fresh alacrity, continued my journey.

I had now got over the common, and was once more in a country rich and well cultivated beyond all conception. This continued to be the case as far as Slough, which is twenty miles and a half from London, on the way to Oxford, and from which to the left there is a road leading to Windsor, whose high white castle I have already seen at a distance. I made no stay here. But went directly to the right, along a very pleasant high road, between meadows and green hedges, towards Windsor, where I arrived about noon. It strikes a foreigner as something un-usual when, on passing through these fine English towns, he observed those circumstances by which the towns in Germany are distinguished from the villages – no walls, no gates, no sentries, nor garrisons. No stern examiner comes here to search and inspects us or our baggage; no imperious guard here demands a sight of our passports; perfectly free and unmolested, we here walk through villages and towns as unconcerned as we should through a house of our own.

Just before I got to Windsor I passed Eton College, one of the first public schools in England, and perhaps in the world. I have before observed that there are in England fewer of these great schools than one might expect. It lay on my left; and on the right directly opposite it was an inn. Into which I went.

I suppose it was during the hour of recreation or playtime when I got to Eton. I saw the boys in the yard before the college, which was enclosed by a low wall, in great numbers, walking and running up and down. Their dress struck me particularly. From the biggest to the least, they all wore black cloaks, or gowns, over coloured clothes, through which there was an aperture for their arms. They also wore a square hat or cap, that seemed to be covered with velvet, such as our clergymen in many places wear. They were differently employed – some talking together, some playing, and some had their books in their hands, and were reading. But I was soon obliged to get out of their sight. They stared at me as I came along, all over with dust, with my stick in my hand.

As I entered the inn and desired to have

something to eat, the countenance of the waiter gave me to understand that I should find no friendly reception. Whatever I got they seemed to give me with such an air that showed how little they thought of me, as if they considered me a beggar. I must do them the justice to own, however, that they suffered me to pay like a gentleman. No doubt this was the first time this pert, be-powdered puppy had ever been called on to wait on a poor devil – who entered their place on foot. I was tired, and asked for a bedroom where I might sleep. They showed me one that resembled a prison for malefactors. I requested that I might have a better room at night, on which, without apology, they told me they had no intention of lodging me, as they had no room for such guests. But I might go back to Slough, where probably I might get a night's lodging.

From 'Travels, Chiefly on Foot, through Several Parts of England in 1782' (translated by the daughter of Charles Godfrey Woide, 1795)

Richard Jefferies

– The Inevitable End of Every Footpath –

A lways get over a stile,' is the one rule that should ever be borne in mind by those who wish to see the land as it really is. That is to say, never omit to explore a footpath, for never was there a footpath yet which did not pass something of interest.

In the meadows, everything comes pressing lovingly up to the path. The small-leaved clover can scarce be driven back by frequent footsteps from endeavouring to cover the bare earth of the centre. Tall buttercups, round whose stalks the cattle have carefully grazed, stand in ranks; strong ox-eye daisies, with broad white disks and torn leaves, form with the grass the tricolour of the pasture white, green, and gold.

When the path enters the mowing-grass, ripe for the scythe, the simplicity of these cardinal hues is lost in the multitude of shades and the addition of other colours. The surface of mowing-grass is indeed made up of so many tints that at the first glance it is confusing; and hence, perhaps, it is that hardly ever has an artist succeeded in getting the effect upon canvas. Of the million blades of grass no two are of the same shade.

Pluck a handful and spread them out side by side and this is at once evident. Nor is any single blade the same shade all the way up. There may be a faint yellow towards the root, a full green about the middle, at the tip perhaps the hot sun has scorched it, and there is a trace of brown. The older grass, which comes up earliest, is distinctly different in tint from that which has but just reached its greatest height, and in which the sap has not yet stood still.

A clouded sky dulls the herbage, a cloudless heaven brightens it, so that the grass almost reflects the firmament like water. At sunset the rosy rays bring out every tint of red or purple. At noonday, watch as alternate shadow and sunshine come one after the other as the clouds are wafted over. By moonlight perhaps the white ox-eyed daisies show the most.

But never will you find the mowing grass in the same field looking twice alike. Come again the day after to-morrow only, and there is a change; some of the grass is riper, some is thicker, with further blades which have pushed up, some browner. Cold northern winds cause it to wear a dry, withered aspect; under warm showers it visibly opens itself; in a hurricane it tosses itself wildly to and fro; it laughs under the sunshine.

There are thick bunches by the footpath, which hang over and brush the feet. While approaching there seems nothing there except grass, but in the act of passing, and thus looking straight down into them, there are blue eyes at the bottom gazing up. These specks of blue sky hidden in the grass tempt the hand to gather them, but then you cannot gather the whole field . . .

Then there are drifting specks of colour which cannot be fixed. Butterflies, white, parti-coloured, brown, and spotted, and light blue flutter along beside the footpath; two white ones wheel about each other, rising higher at every turn till they are lost and no more to be distinguished against a shining white cloud.

Large dark humble bees roam slowly, and honey bees with more decided flight. Glistening beetles, green and gold, run across the bare earth of the path, coming from one crack in the dry ground and disappearing in the (to them) mighty chasm of another.

Tiny green 'hoppers' odd creatures shaped something like the fancy frogs of children's storybooks alight upon it after a spring, and pausing a second, with another toss themselves as high as the highest bennet (veritable elm-trees by comparison), to fall anywhere out of sight in the grass. Reddish ants hurry over. Time is money; and their business brooks no delay.

Bee-like flies of many stripes and parti-coloured robes face you, suspended in the air with wings vibrating so swiftly as to be unseen; then suddenly jerk themselves a few yards, to recommence hovering.

A greenfinch rises with a yellow gleam and a sweet note from the grass, and is off with something for his brood, or a starling, solitary now, for his mate is in the nest, startled from his questing, goes straight away.

Dark starlings, greenfinch, gilded fly, glistening beetle, blue butterfly, humble bee with scarf about his thick waist, add their moving dots of colour to the surface. There is no design, no balance, nothing like a pattern perfect on the right-hand side, and exactly equal on the left-hand. Even trees which have some semblance of balance in form are not really so, and as you walk round them so their outline changes.

Now the path approaches a stile set deep in thorns and brambles, and hardly to be gained for curved hooks and prickles. But on the briars June roses bloom, arches of flowers over nettles, burdock, and rushes in the ditch beneath. Sweet roses buds yet unrolled, white and conical; roses half open and pink tinted; roses widespread, the petals curling backwards on the hedge, abandoning their beauty to the sun. In the pasture over the stile a roan cow feeds unmoved, calmly content, gathering the grass with rough tongue. It is not only what you actually see along the path, but what you remember to have seen, that gives it its beauty.

From hence the path skirts the hedge enclosing

a copse, part of which had been cut in the winter, so that a few weeks since in spring the bluebells could be seen, instead of being concealed by the ash branches and the woodbine. Among them grew one with white bells, like a lily, solitary in the midst of the azure throng. A ' drive', or green lane passing between the ash-stoles, went into the copse, with tufts of tussocky grass on either side and rush bunches, till further away the overhanging branches, where the poles were uncut, hid its course.

Already the grass has hidden the ruts left by the timber carriages – the last came by on May Day with ribbons of orange, red, and blue on the horses' heads for honour of the day. Another, which went past in the wintry weeks of the early year, was drawn by a team wearing the ancient harness with bells under high hoods, or belfries, bells well attuned, too, and not far inferior to those rung by handbell men. The beat of the three horses' hoofs sounds like the drum that marks time to the chime upon their backs. Seldom even in the far away country, can that pleasant chime be heard . . .

It was near this copse that in early spring I stayed to gather some white sweet violets, for the true wild violet is very nearly white. I stood close to a hedger and ditcher, who, standing on a board, was cleaning out the mud that the water might run freely. He went on with his work, taking not the least notice of an idler, but intent upon his labour, as a good and true man should be. But when I spoke to him he answered me in clear, well-chosen language, well pronounced, 'in good set terms'.

No slurring of consonants and broadening of vowels, no involved and backward construction depending on the listener's previous knowledge for comprehension, no half sentences indicating rather than explaining, but correct sentences. With his shoes almost covered by the muddy water, his hands black and grimy, his brown face splashed with mud, leaning on his shovel he stood and talked from the deep ditch, not much more than head and shoulders visible above it. It seemed a voice from the very earth, speaking of education, change, and possibilities.

The copse is now filling up with undergrowth; the brambles are spreading, the briars extending, masses of nettles, and thistles like saplings in size and height, crowding the spaces between the ash-stoles. By the banks great cow-parsnips or 'gix' have opened their broad heads of white flowers; teazles have lifted themselves into view, every opening is occupied. There is a scent of elder flowers, the meadowsweet is pushing up, and will soon be out, and an odour of new-mown hay floats on the breeze.

From hence the footpath, leaving the copse, descends into a hollow, with a streamlet flowing through a little meadow, barely an acre, with a pollard oak in the centre, the rising ground on two sides shutting out all but the sky, and on the third another wood. Such a dreamy hollow might be painted for a glade in the Forest of Arden, and there on the sward and leaning against the ancient oak one might read the play through without being disturbed by a single passer by. A few steps further and the stile opens on a road.

There the teams travel with rows of brazen spangles down their necks, some with a wheatsheaf for design, some with a swan. The road itself, if you follow it, dips into a valley where the horses must splash through the water of a brook spread out some fifteen or twenty yards wide; for, after the primitive Surrey fashion, there is no bridge for wagons. A narrow wooden structure bears foot-passengers; you cannot but linger half across and look down into its clear stream. Up the current where it issues from the fields and falls over a slight obstacle, the sunlight plays and glances.

A great hawthorn bush grows on the bank; in spring, white with May; in autumn, red with haws or peggles. To the shallow shore of the brook, where it washes the flints and moistens the dust, the housemartins come for mortar. A constant succession of birds arrive all day long to drink at the clear stream, often alighting on the fragments of chalk and flint which stand in the water, and are to them as rocks.

Another footpath leads from the road across

the meadows to where the brook is spanned by the strangest bridge, built of brick, with one arch, but only just wide enough for a single person to walk, and with parapets only four or five inches high. It is thrown aslant the stream, and not straight across it, and has a long brick approach. It is not unlike on a small scale the bridges seen in views of Eastern travel. Another path leads to a hamlet, consisting of a church, a farmhouse, and three or four cottages – a veritable hamlet in every sense of the word.

In a village a few miles distant, as you walk between cherry and pear orchards, you pass a little shop the sweets, and twine, and trifles are such as may be seen in similar windows a hundred miles distant. There is the very wooden measure for nuts, which has been used time out of mind, in the distant country. Out again into the road as the sun sinks, and westwards the wind lifts a cloud of dust, which is lit up and made rosy by the rays passing through it. For such is the beauty of the sunlight that it can impart a glory even to dust.

Once more, never go by a stile (that does not look private) without getting over it and following the path. But they all end in one place. After rambling across furze and heath, or through dark fir woods; after lingering in the meadows among the buttercups, or by the copses where the pheasants crow; after gathering June roses, or, in later days, staining the lips with blackberries or cracking nuts, by-and-by the path brings you in sight of a railway station. And the railway station, through some process of mind, presently compels you to go up on the platform, and after a little puffing and revolution of wheels you emerge at Charing-cross, or London Bridge, or Waterloo, or Ludgate-hill, and, with the freshness of the meadows still clinging to your coat, mingle with the crowd.

The inevitable end of every footpath round about London is London.

All paths go thither.

If it were far away in the distant country you might sit down in the shadow upon the hay and fall asleep, or dream awake hour after hour. There would be no inclination to move. But if you sat down on the sward under the ancient pollard oak in the little mead with the brook, and the wood of which I spoke just now as like a glade in the enchanted Forest of Arden, this would not be possible.

It is the proximity of the immense City which induces a mental, a nerve restlessness. As you sit and would dream a something plucks at the mind with constant reminder; you cannot dream for long, you must up and away, and, turn in which direction you please, ultimately it will lead you to London.

From *Nature Near London*, 1883

James Boswell

– A Good Deal Odoriferous –

Mr Johnson and I walked arm-in-arm up the high street, to my house in James Court: I could not prevent his being assailed by the evening affluvia of Edinburgh. I heard a late baronet, of some distinction in the political world in the beginning of the present reign, observe, that 'walking the streets of Edinburgh at night was pretty perilous and a good deal odoriferous'. The peril is much abated by the care with which the city magistrates have taken to enforce the city laws against throwing foul water from the windows; but, from the structures of the houses in old town, which consist of many stories, in each of which a different family lives, and there being no covered sewers, the odour still continues. A zealous Scotsman would have wished Mr Johnson to be without one of his five senses on this occasion. As we marched slowly along, he grumbled in my ear, 'I smell you in the dark!' but he acknowledged that the breadth of the street, and the loftiness of the buildings on each side, made a noble appearance . . .

From *Journal of a Tour to the Hebrides*, 1785

Fanny Kemble

– Shouting Children –

At seven o'clock, D and I walked out together. The evening was very beautiful, and we walked as far as Canal Street and back. During our promenade, two fire-engines passed us, attended by the usual retinue of shouting children; this is about the sixth fire since yesterday evening. They are so frequent here, that the cry 'Fire, fire!' seems to excite neither alarm nor curiosity, and except the above-mentioned pains-taking juveniles, none of the inhabitants seem in the least disturbed by it. We prosecuted our walk clown to the Battery, but just as we reached it we had to return, as it was tea-time. I was sorry: the whole scene was most lovely.

From *Mrs Butler's Diary*, 1835

Edward Hoagland

– Don't Bleed on Me –

T here is a time of life somewhere between
the sullen fugues of adolescence and the
retrenchments of middle age when human nature
becomes so absolutely absorbing one wants to be
in the city constantly, even at the height of summer.
Nature can't seem to hold a candle to it. One
gobbles the blocks, and if the weather is sweaty, so
much the better; it brings everybody else out too.
To the enthusiast's eye, what might later look to be
human avarice is simply energy, brutality is strength,
ambition is not wearisome or repellent or even
alarming. In my own case, aiming to be a writer, I
knew that every mile I walked, the better writer I'd
be; and I went to Twentieth Street and the Hudson
River to smell the yeasty redolence of the Nabisco
factory, and to West Twelfth Street to sniff the police
stables. In the meat-market district nearby, if a tyro
complained that his back ached, the saying was
'don't bleed on me'...

Oh yes, oh yes! One says, revisiting these old
walking neighbourhoods. Yorkville, Inwood,
Columbus Avenue. Our New York sky is not
muscular with cloud formations as is San Francisco's,
or as green-smelling as London's, and rounding a

corner here, one doesn't stop stock-still to gaze at the buildings as in Venice. The bartenders like to boast that in this city we have the 'best and worst', yet intelligent conversation, for example, is mostly ad-libbed and comes in fits and starts, anywhere or nowhere; one cannot trot out of an evening and go looking for it. We have our famous New York energy instead, as well as its reverse, which is the keening misery, the special New York craziness, as if every thirteenth person standing on the street is wearing a gauzy hospital smock and paper shower slippers.

'City Walking', 1975

Christopher Hope

– Traffic Torrential –

S ome of the special pleasures the city has to offer are the sort you might as well enjoy because they are unavoidable. Take crossing the street in the Old Quarter. This you do by lifting your elbows high, as if fording a furious stream. The street is narrow but the traffic torrential. The trick is to walk forward slowly enough for drivers to see you in time to avoid you, but fast enough to gain the centre without being knocked down. Then, with a quick glance left and right, the same deliberate steps carry you on the other side. It is an enormous thrill, like white water rafting. The important thing is to take the plunge. I've seen tourists standing for ten minutes staring into the hurtling traffic, unable to put a toe into the stream, hoping perhaps that the flood will stop. But it never stops.

From *The Hanoi Hug*, 1998

Kamila Shamsie

– Trepidation –

When had I last walked alone anywhere past midnight, or at the break of day? Perhaps on my way home from the tube station, alert to footfalls, walking fast to stave off not cold but strangers. In Karachi, where I grew up, I would never do this. By 'this' I meant not the walk itself, but the walk without trepidation. A woman walking alone after midnight is always too conscious of being alone to properly inhabit that space which is solitude.

From 'Winterwalks', 2008

George Sand

– No Need to Hurry –

(i)

I n those days, I crudely called it my life as a
street Arab, and there was indeed a residue of
aristocratic mockery in the way I pictured it; for
actually my character was taking shape and real life
was opening up before, dressed as I was in men's
clothing, which allowed me to be enough of a man
to see a milieu that otherwise would have remained
forever closed to the bumpkin I had been until then.

(ii)

So I had a 'sentry box redingote' made for myself,
out of thick gray cloth, with matching trousers and
vest. With a gray hat and a wide wool tie, I was the
perfect little first year student. I cannot tell you the
pleasure I derived from my boots – I would gladly
have slept in them, as my brother did in his youth,
when he put on his first pair. With those little iron
heels, I felt secure on the sidewalks. I flew from
one end of Paris to the other. It seemed to me I
could have made a trip around the world. Also, my
clothing made me fearless. I was on the go in all kinds
of weather, I came in at all hours . . . no one paid
attention to me, no one suspected my disguise. Aside

from the fact that I wore it with ease, the absence of coquettishness in costume and facial expression warded off any suspicion. I was too poorly dressed and looked too simple – my usual vacant, verging on dumb, look – to attract or compel attention. Women understand very little about wearing a disguise . . .

(iii)

My own ideal was lodged in a corner of my brain, and I needed only a few days of complete freedom to have it blossom. I carried it with me into the street, my feet on the icy patches, my shoulders covered with snow, my hands in my pockets, my stomach a little empty sometimes, but my head all the more filled with dreams, melodies, colours, shapes, lights, and phantom figures. I was no longer a lady, nor was I a 'gentleman'. I was jostled on the sidewalk like a thing that got in the way of busy passers-by. I didn't care; I wasn't busy . . . in Paris, no one thought anything at all about me. I had no need to hurry in order to avoid banalities; I could create a whole novel going from one end of town to another without meeting anyone who would ask me, 'What the devil has you so engrossed?' That was worth more than a convent cell. And I could have said with satisfaction what Rene said with sadness – I am walking in a 'desert of men'.

From *Story of My Life*, 1854 (group translation, edited by Thelma Jurgrau, 1991)

Lauren Elkin

– A Dawdling Observer –

I remember when I'd take the metro two stops because I didn't realize how close together everything was, how walkable Paris was. I had to walk around to understand where I was in space, how places related to each other. Some days I'd cover five miles or more, returning home with sore feet and a story or two for my room-mates. I saw things I'd never seen in New York. Beggars (Roma, I was told) who knelt rigidly in the street, heads bowed, holding signs asking for money, some with children, some with dogs; homeless people living in tents, under stairways, under arches. Every quaint Parisian nook had its corresponding misery. I turned off my New York apathy and gave what I could. Learning to see meant not being able to look away; to walk in the streets of Paris was to walk the thin line of fate that divided us from each other.

And then somehow, by chance, I learned that all that walking around, feeling intensely, constantly moved to scribble what I saw and felt into floppy notebooks I bought at the St Michel bookstore Gilbert Jeune – all that I did instinctively, others had done to such an extent that there was a word for it. I was a *flaneur.*

Or rather – a good student of French, I converted the masculine noun to a feminine one – a *flaneuse*.

Flaneuse (flanne-euhze), noun from the French. Feminine form of *flaneur (flanne-euhr),* an idler, a dawdling observer, usually found in cities.

This is an imaginary definition. Most French dictionaries don't even include the word. The 1905 *Littré* does make an allowance for *'flaneur, -euse'. Qui flane.* But the *Dictionnaire Vivant de la Langue Francaise* defines it, believe it or not, as a kind of lounge chair.

Is that some kind of joke? The only kind of curious idling a woman does is lying down?

This usage (slang of course) began around 1840 and peaked in the 1920s, but continues today: search for 'flaneuse' on Google Images and the word brings up a drawing of George Sand, a picture of a young woman sitting on a Parisian bench and a few images of outdoor furniture.

From *Flaneuse*, 2016

Virginia Woolf

– Between Tea and Dinner –

N o one perhaps has ever felt passionately towards
a lead pencil. But there are circumstances in
which it can become supremely desirable to possess
one; moments when we are set upon having an
object, an excuse for walking half across London
between tea and dinner. As the foxhunter hunts in
order to preserve the breed of foxes, and the golfer
plays in order that open spaces may be preserved
from the builders, so when the desire comes upon us
to go street rambling the pencil does for a pretext,
and getting up we say: 'Really I must buy a pencil,'
as if under cover of this excuse we could indulge
safely in the greatest pleasure of town life in winter
– rambling the streets of London.

The hour should be the evening and the season
winter, for in winter the champagne brightness of
the air and the sociability of the streets are grateful.
We are not then taunted as in the summer by the
longing for shade and solitude and sweet airs from
the hayfields. The evening hour, too, gives us the
irresponsibility which darkness and lamplight
bestow. We are no longer quite ourselves. As we
step out of the house on a fine evening between
four and six, we shed the self our friends know us

by and become part of that vast republican army of anonymous trampers, whose society is so agreeable after the solitude of one's own room. For there we sit surrounded by objects which perpetually express the oddity of our own temperaments and enforce the memories of our own experience . . .

But when the door shuts on us, all that vanishes. The shell-like covering which our souls have excreted to house themselves, to make for themselves a shape distinct from others, is broken, and there is left of all these wrinkles and roughnesses a central oyster of perceptiveness, an enormous eye. How beautiful a street is in winter! It is at once revealed and obscured. Here vaguely one can trace symmetrical straight avenues of doors and windows; here under the lamps are floating islands of pale light through which pass quickly bright men and women, who, for all their poverty and shabbiness, wear a certain look of unreality, an air of triumph, as if they had given life the slip, so that life, deceived of her prey, blunders on without them. But, after all, we are only gliding smoothly on the surface. The eye is not a miner, not a diver, not a seeker after buried treasure. It floats us smoothly down a stream; resting, pausing, the brain sleeps perhaps as it looks.

How beautiful a London street is then, with its islands of light, and its long groves of darkness, and on one side of it perhaps some tree-sprinkled, grass-grown space where night is folding herself to sleep naturally and, as one passes the iron railing, one hears those little cracklings and stirrings of leaf and twig which seem to suppose the silence of fields all round them, an owl hooting, and far away the rattle of a train in the valley. But this is London, we are reminded; high among the bare trees are hung oblong frames of reddish yellow light – windows; there are points of brilliance burning steadily like low stars – lamps; this empty ground, which holds the country in it and its peace, is only a London square, set about by offices and houses where at this hour fierce lights burn over maps, over documents, over desks where clerks sit turning with wetted forefinger the files of endless correspondences; or more suffusedly the firelight wavers and the lamplight falls upon the privacy of some drawing-room, its easy chairs, its papers, its china, its inlaid table, and the figure of a woman, accurately measuring out the precise number of spoons of tea which— She looks at the door as if she heard a ring downstairs and somebody asking, is she in?

But here we must stop peremptorily. We are in danger of digging deeper than the eye approves; we are impeding our passage down the smooth stream by catching at some branch or root. At any moment, the sleeping army may stir itself and wake in us a thousand violins and trumpets in response; the army of human beings may rouse itself and assert all its oddities and sufferings and sordidities. Let us dally a little longer, be content still with surfaces only – the glossy brilliance of the motor omnibuses; the carnal splendour of the butchers' shops with their yellow flanks and purple steaks; the blue and red bunches of flowers burning so bravely through the plate glass of the florists' windows.

For the eye has this strange property: it rests only on beauty; like a butterfly it seeks colour and basks in warmth. On a winter's night like this, when nature has been at pains to polish and preen herself, it brings back the prettiest trophies, breaks off little lumps of emerald and coral as if the whole earth were made of precious stone. The thing it cannot do (one is speaking of the average unprofessional eye) is to compose these trophies in such a way as to bring out the more obscure angles and relationships.

Passing, glimpsing, everything seems accidentally but miraculously sprinkled with beauty, as if the tide of trade which deposits its burden so punctually and prosaically upon the shores of Oxford Street had this night cast up nothing but treasure. With no thought of buying, the eye is sportive and generous; it creates; it adorns; it enhances. Standing out in the street, one may build up all the chambers of an imaginary house and furnish them at one's will with sofa, table, carpet. That rug will do for the hall. That alabaster bowl shall stand on a carved table in the window. Our merrymaking shall be reflected in that thick round mirror. But, having built and furnished the house, one is happily under no obligation to possess it; one can dismantle it in the twinkling of an eye, and build and furnish another house with other chairs and other glasses. Or let us indulge ourselves at the antique jewellers, among the trays of rings and the hanging necklaces. Let us choose those pearls, for example, and then imagine how, if we put them on, life would be changed. It becomes instantly between two and three in the morning; the lamps are burning very white in the deserted streets of Mayfair. Only motor-cars are abroad at this hour, and one has a sense of emptiness, of airiness, of secluded gaiety. Wearing pearls, wearing silk, one steps out on to a balcony which overlooks the gardens of sleeping Mayfair. There are a few lights in the bedrooms of great peers returned from Court, of silk-stockinged footmen, of dowagers who have pressed the hands of statesmen. A cat creeps along the garden wall. Love-making is going on sibilantly, seductively in the darker places of the room behind thick green curtains. Strolling sedately as if he were promenading a terrace beneath which the shires and counties of England lie sun-bathed, the aged Prime Minister recounts to Lady So-and–So with the curls and the emeralds the true history of some great crisis in the affairs of the land. We seem to be riding on the top of the highest mast of the tallest ship; and yet at the same time we know that nothing of this sort matters; love is not proved thus, nor great achievements completed thus; so that we sport with the moment and preen our feathers in it lightly, as we stand on the balcony watching the moonlit cat creep along Princess Mary's garden wall.

But what could be more absurd? It is, in fact, on the stroke of six; it is a winter's evening; we are walking to the Strand to buy a pencil . . .

From 'Street Haunting: A London Adventure', 1930

Will Self

– Is This a Real City? –

J oachim Schlor in his seminal study *Nights in the Big City* writes how the coming of street lighting, to Western cities in the mid-nineteenth century, was attended by an upsurge in moral panic. Far from experiencing the illumination as the banishment of infernal darkness, many burghers perceived a dangerous and unnatural phenomenon. The lit-up city was a realm within which the established divisions between interior and exterior were broken down: no longer did the good citizen lock up his door at nightfall, and wait for the cock's crow.

By the same token, street lighting allowed for the mingling of classes and sexes in new and promiscuous ways – so nightlife was born. The ability to move easily about the city, traversing zones heretofore off-limits and penetrating sequestered neighbourhoods, crystallised urban self-consciousness. The city dwellers were now permanently checking themselves in the lit windows of shops, and seeing there, imprisoned, Escher-like, their own reflection and the images of that which they desired.

Even in our own era, a hundred and forty years later, the city by night still appears as a distinctively modern terrain: at once minatory and compelling, too bright and too obscure. The shadows are sharply adumbrated, the colours are leeched out, the people stroll, hurry and lurk, players on a stage set that has been erected For One Night Only.

Any serious *flaneur* walks by night as much as by day; for by day it's too easy to be drawn into a complacent acceptance of normalcy. This much we plainly know: the panel truck disgorging toilet paper; the smoking secretary with laddered tights; the dosser senatorial, sporting a sleeping bag for a toga. But by night these are shapeshifters, capable of defeating our expectations. They may assume the faces of loved ones, and so effortlessly enforce intimacy – or seem strange to the point of being alien, and so provoke repulsion. We may fancy ourselves rational and civilised, yet immediately beyond the sodium firelight, the wolves are always pacing the paving stones.

I walk by night. I remember years ago, before there were buses or tubes on New Year's Eve, walking over London Bridge, in the chill of the first 3 a.m. of the year, and seeing an entire platoon of Roman Legionnaires come marching towards me. At the front a standard bearer carried the Eagle captioned 'SPQR', at the back a drummer in a leopard skin beat the rhythm for their sandaled feet.

I was not alone, so could not dismiss this as fancy or hallucination. Yet, neither my companions nor I, were disposed to talk to each other as the ancient squad passed us by; nor did we hail them, nor did we speak of it again. It was a benison of the night.

I have trudged through the dust of Varanasi in Uttar Pradesh, by the forty watt-lighted sheds, where everything mechanical that can be dismantled is bolted together again; and by the candle-guttering hovels, where women knead chapatti dough as dun as the walls of their own, malleable dwellings.

In the heat of the night cities exhale: ghee sizzles and releases the food smells into the dark, where human minds, starved of vision, open up their nostrils to see. By night all hot cities are synaesthetic, in this way: scrambling up sound and smell and touch, so that a milk train, clacking over points, feels up your spine with metallic fingertips.

I have walked uptown from the Village, on Halloween night, passing by the raggedy company of ghoulish New Yorkers, all Gothed-up in Gotham, their eyes black-rimmed, their teeth bloodstained. We were carrying our eldest son, then a newborn baby, and Morticia after Cruella stopped to bill and coo: 'Is that a real baby?'

Is this a real city? was the only possible rejoinder. In the chill darkness New York forfeits any claim on our amazement. The pinprick lights of the vertiginous towers merge with the empyrean itself, while at ground level, fire hydrant after phone booth after Korean corner shop provide the delusions of human scale. It's all about *us*, isn't it? Along the long ramps of the avenue, taxis wallow, their grimacing fenders gulp up the devilish steam clouds escaping from manholes, then their trunks release them in vaporous gouts.

But tonight I'm not in the east or the south or the west, not in Varanasi or London or New York, I'm in Glasgow, dining with the writer Alasdair Gray and his wife, Morag. I'm not thinking about night walking especially. We're sitting in the brasserie of the Óran Mor, the arts centre on the corner of Byres Road and the Great Western. Upstairs, on the ceiling of the enormous nave – it was once a Presbyterian church with a pituitary disorder – Alasdair has painted one of his distinctive murals: Zodiacal figures striking hieratic attitudes against the vaulted blue sky.

There is the deep blue of the night sky in his mural, and Alasdair and his co-workers have scattered silvery stars across it. Of course, the anti-naturalism of this is all the more poignant in the heart of the city, where the constant haemorrhaging of electric light bleeds sodium into the darkness. We use different parts of the eye – rods and cones – with which to see colour; at night, in the absence of electric light, we see the world in a ghostly monochrome; or rather, we see it in a beautiful, silver nitrate monochrome, if only we allow it to swim out of the dark fluid for us: night sight takes time to develop – at least a half hour. Instead of this ulterior vision, the city the splashes Day-Glo red, blue and orange across our eyes, and it's only in their lurid afterimages that we become creepily aware: the silhouette of the beast remains in the shadows.

Alasdair is speaking of Flann O'Brien and a conceit that he particularly likes in *The Third Policeman*: 'You recall,' he squeak-says, in his distinctively staccato manner, alternating between parody and self-parody, 'the character of, um, de Selby, and his, ah, theory that night, far from being darkness, is, in fact, a *morbid exhalation* of some kind: "black air". De Selby didn't *know* that much about the, um, black air, although he had reached the conclusion – following certain *ex-per-i-ments*, that it must be a gas – because when he lit a candle, it burned, and the black air, ah, *dissipated*!'

Alasdair's words inspire me, and I decide to walk back to my hotel, the Hilton at Charing Cross. I like to stay at the Hilton when I'm in Glasgow, a tower block of faux-domesticity by the M8 flyover, from its prow-shaped windows it offers the biggest views out over the valley of the Clyde, or out towards its mouth, or north, into the hills at Mingavie. I can't sleep well in hotels: sleep is too big a descent into the black air with nothing familiar around you. The French have it wrong, it isn't orgasm that's the 'little death', but sleep – even an afternoon nap in a hotel is a micro-extinction for me. In the severe rationality of the Hilton's shoebox rooms, the owlish visitor, alone and sick of the TV lightbox, can turn his attention outwards, and imagine himself flying up into the sky, buffeted by grey Zeppelins of cloud, their undersides bilious from the street lighting.

India, seen by night from high above, is a diadem of a subcontinent, jewelled by the faint gleam of its myriad villages scattered regularly across the Gangetic plain. The lambency of the earth's cities is visible from space: a Cosmonaut, or an American billionaire, who steps out from the Mir space station for a short walk, must find himself stroll-orbiting on this pavement of lights. A 20,000 mph constitutional from the few remaining dark patches of the world – its increasingly tepid poles, and equatorial bald spots – to the mighty blaze of Western Europe, the east and western seaboards of North America, where untold ergs of energy are hurled skyward: Zeus's thunderbolts returned to him with a vengeance.

I say goodbye to Alasdair and Morag and leave. Suddenly, I'm standing outside the brasserie looking at a man with a fighter-pilot moustache, who's leaning, smoking, against a steel bollard. It's a chilly night in the north, and we've been forced to acquire the habit of exile, along with our other one. The transition from interior to exterior is that much more extreme by night. Thrust into the chill and unsettling city, what could be more understandable than the newly primitive desire to light a small fire and warm your lips round it? He stares balefully over at me, his fighter must look like an enormous cigarette – so nicotininious is his facial hair.

'Why've they put 'em there?' He grunts, jerking a thumb at some metal tables and chairs outside the adjoining pub.

'I imagine they're looking forward to the summer,' I say. He grinds out his butt and comes up to impress his walrus muzzle on me:

'Oh, aye,' he groans. 'Mebbe.'

'It's the triumph,' I say, sententiously, 'of hope over expectation.'

This pricks his interest and he peers at me with watery-eyed gratitude. Looking at his saggy denim arse as he shuffles back into the pub, it occurs to me that this may be the first time in weeks that anyone has addressed him as if he possesses a brain not sodden.

I set off to walk the two or three miles back to my hotel. It's that paradoxical time of year, poised on the cusp of spring, when some urbanites huddle up while others strip off. To some, the night is a velvet cloak to be draped around their bare shoulders, to others it's black ice insinuated between stubbly neck and furry collar. By a post office box a waif stands with her chapped lips riveted together, and the bright pink stippling of goose bumps on her white, white calves.

I think of long evenings when summer is

finally here. In London, where I live, there are no Dostoevskian 'white nights', such as you get here in the north; instead, the heat seems to build into the dusk, a mounting rhythm as all the exhaust fumes, rubber, leather and grease pounded into the paving stones and tarmac reach a critical mass, before exhaling into the cooling air. At those times, walking back from the West End, seeing the strollers on the Embankment in shorts and T-shirts, or the clones outside the Vauxhall Tavern, shaven-headed and bare-chested, the night-time city is a boudoir, with its sexed-up inhabitants in increasing states of *déshabillé*.

I head away from the main road, up glistening pavements between privet hedges. There's the faintest of mizzles, a percolation of water into the air, so that in the downlight of the streetlamps, sparkly, diaphanous curtains waver and distort. The houses are large and handsome; their porticos are rendered in stone and supported by Grecian pillars. Urns and petrified laurel wreaths are poised on head-height gateposts. Through the clear panes of one sash window I see a couple, a wine bottle, incendiary news footage on a television by the fireplace. I covet their framed art exhibition posters, their tufted rug, their family photos more than anything I've ever wanted before. Nothing and nobody is more covetable than a cosy dwelling, seen by night from the street without. The sash window is a shop window and what's for sale here is an idea of cosy homeliness that can never be experienced, except by a voyeur.

On I plod, past the unutterable gloom of a silent, suburban church, down an alleyway and back on to the main road. The parked cars are now pearlised with raindrops; a take-out chef kneels to close his shop grille with a rattle; the enlarged photos in the furniture store are portraits of the ideal – yet absent – family that lives here. There are also pubs and shops along this paving stone strand, young people stand out in the street, smoking and drinking from clear bottles full of some fluid rendered bilious by the sodium glare of the streetlamps. I'm entering their territory, and everything in their body language – the way they butt and rut, the way they preen and keen – suggests that they guard it zealously. Yet, I'm invisible, beneath my own magical cloak of middle age. By day strangers can be scrutinised, by night we are reduced to the crudest approximations: age, gender, height, bulk, and dismissed accordingly.

Turning down another quiet street – this time one lined by the flat facades of two-up, two-down terraced houses – I'm discomfited by the presence of a fellow night walker; a woman, trim and well-dressed, who clacks along the pavement on high heels. I feel that dreadful sense of *reverse paranoia* that always comes upon me when I find myself walking behind a single woman by night; and this time, as I am in a melancholy mood, it's intensified. Night walking is a luxury for a man such as myself, too old to attract casual aggro, too large to be easy prey. It's worth remembering that for many others the night-time city is a genuine jungle, not merely a psychic adventure playground.

At the next corner the orange wash of artificial light and the brown miasma of the shadows, is slashed apart by the revolving blue blades that coruscate from the roof of a police car. Two officers stand either side of a rubbish bag full of humanity that's draped over a garden wall. Their fluorescent jackets give them the appearance of plastic bafflers arranged around a traffic accident. The cheap jewellery of broken glass lies scattered on the pavement at their feet.

I'm relieved by the presence of the police – it damps down my reverse paranoia. The woman ahead of us fumbles in her handbag for her key, and opens the front door of the house next door. I pass by, ignored by all. Come dawn, all that will be left of this incident are the contents of an abused stomach fertilising an herbaceous border. Oh! Those herbaceous borders, those privet hedges flocculent and strong-smelling by night, more bucolic than any country lane.

Then, a grand building, A huge, elongated dome, two L-shaped wings bracket a courtyard, and flap away the night. It takes me what seem like aeons to proceed along its frontage, beside its punitive iron railings, under the stare of its hundreds of blank windows. Then, quite suddenly, we can see the city spread out below and to our right, a sparking grid of streets; while ahead, the motorway flyover strides on blocky concrete legs, its deck swishing with speedy, late-night traffic.

By night, the underside of the flyover is a cloistral space – but writ unbelievably large. I decide to work my way down the slip road, past behemoth Indian restaurants, and go underneath it on to a patch of wasteland. This – it occurs to me, as I struggle over mounds of shattered masonry and through inappropriate thistle patches – is the real temple of modernity. This is the city's Baalbec, with its bulbous pillars, its Byzantine illuminations, its altar of traffic lights. I remember being in San Francisco, a few months after the earthquake, and walking by night beside a flyover such as this, but one buckled and broken. It felt like a total reversal of civilisation, a halting progress back to the primeval.

A scamper across the slip road, a traverse across a car park, up a ramp, and there it is: the bland uniformity of the hotel, rising up twenty storeys, each lighted window another desperate little tale. The electric doors whoosh open and I'm yanked into the lobby. Even though I've only been walking for an hour, it's enough to completely destabilise me. In here, everything is too close up, too in-yer-face, too large and bright and insistent. Shaven-headed businessman bouncers stand on a quarter-acre of carpet, giving each other strong-arm handshakes, breaking into one another's personality.

Our ancestors were right it seems, to fear the lighting of the city; for, by banishing the night from the outside, we've sucked it into our own interiors.

'Nightwalks', 2007

Robert Louis Stevenson

– I Must Camp –

'Sir,' said I, with my most commanding manners, 'you are a coward.'

And with that I turned my back upon the family party, who hastened to retire within their fortifications; and the famous door was closed again, but not till I had overheard the sound of laughter. *Filia barbara pater barbarior.* Let me say it in the plural: the Beasts of Gévaudan.

The lanterns had somewhat dazzled me, and I ploughed distressfully among stones and rubbish heaps. All the other houses in the village were both dark and silent; and though I knocked at here and there a door, my knocking was unanswered. It was a bad business. I gave up Fouzilhac with my curses. The rain had stopped, and the wind, which still kept rising, began to dry my coat and trousers. 'Very well,' thought I, 'water or no water, I must camp.' But the first thing was to return to Modestine. I am pretty sure I was twenty minutes groping for my lady in the dark; arid if it had not been for the unkindly services of the bog, into which I once more stumbled, I might have still been groping for her at the dawn. My next business was to gain the shelter of a wood, for the wind was cold as well as boisterous. How, in this well-wooded district, I should have been so long in finding one, is another of the insoluble mysteries of this day's adventures; but I will take my oath that I put near an hour to the discovery.

At last black trees began to show upon my left, and, suddenly crossing the road, made a cave of unmitigated blackness right in front. I call it a cave without exaggeration; to pass below that arch of leaves was like entering a dungeon. I felt about until my hand encountered a stout branch; and to this I tied Modestine, a haggard, drenched, desponding donkey. Then I lowered my pack, laid it along the wall on the margin of the road, and unbuckled the straps. I knew well enough where the lantern was; but where were the candles? I groped and groped among the tumbled articles, and, while I was thus groping, suddenly I touched the spirit-lamp. Salvation! This would serve my turn as well. The wind roared unwearyingly among the trees; I could hear the boughs tossing and the leaves churning through half a mile of forest; yet the scene of my encampment was not only as black as the pit, but admirably sheltered. At the second match the wick caught flame. The light was both livid and shifting; but it cut me off from the universe, and doubled the darkness of the surrounding night.

I tied Modestine more conveniently for herself, and broke up half the black bread for her supper, reserving the other half against the morning. Then

I gathered what I should want within reach, took off my wet boots and gaiters, which I wrapped in my waterproof, arranged my knapsack for a pillow under the flap of my sleeping-bag, insinuated my limbs into the interior, and buckled myself in like a bambino. I opened a tin of Bologna sausage and broke a cake of chocolate, and that was all I had to eat. It may sound offensive, but I ate them together, bite by bite, by way of bread and meat. All I had to wash down this revolting mixture was neat brandy: a revolting beverage in itself. But I was rare and hungry; ate well, and smoked one of the best cigarettes in my experience. Then I put a stone in my straw hat, pulled the flap of my fur cap over my neck and eyes, put my revolver ready to my hand, and snuggled well down among the sheepskins.

I questioned at first if I were sleepy, for I felt my heart beating faster than usual, as if with an agreeable excitement to which my mind remained a stranger. But as soon as my eyelids touched, that subtle glue leaped between them, and they would no more come separate.

The wind among the trees was my lullaby. Sometimes it sounded for minutes together with a steady even rush, not rising nor abating; and again it would swell and burst like a great crashing breaker, and the trees would patter me all over with big drops from the rain of the afternoon. Night after night, in my own bedroom in the country, I have given ear to this perturbing concert of the wind among the woods; but whether it was a difference in the trees, or the lie of the ground, or because I was myself outside and in the midst of it, the fact remains that the wind sang to a different tune among these woods of Gévaudan. I hearkened and hearkened; and meanwhile sleep took gradual possession of my body and subdued my thoughts and senses; but still my last waking effort was to listen and distinguish, and my last conscious state was one of wonder at the foreign clamour in my ears.

Twice in the course of the dark hours – once when a stone galled me underneath the sack, and again when the poor patient Modestine, growing angry, pawed and stamped upon the road – I was recalled for a brief while to consciousness, and saw a star or two overhead, and the lace-like edge of the foliage against the sky. When I awoke for the third time (Wednesday, September 25th), the world was flooded with a blue light. I saw the leaves labouring in the wind and the ribbon of the road; and, on turning my head, there was Modestine tied to a beech, and standing half across the path in an attitude of inimitable patience. I closed my eyes again, and set to thinking over the experience of the night. I was surprised to find how easy and pleasant it had been, even in this tempestuous weather.

From *Travels With My Donkey*, 1875

Franz Kafka

– In a Sudden Access of Restlessness –

When it seems we have finally decided to stay home of an evening, have slipped into our smoking jackets, are sitting at a lit table after supper, and have taken out some piece of work or game at the conclusion of which we customarily go to bed, when the weather outside is inclement, which makes it perfectly understandable that we are staying at home, when we have been sitting quietly at our table for so long that our going out would provoke general astonishment, when the stairwell is dark and the front gate is bolted, and when, in spite of it all, in a sudden access of restlessness, we get up, change into a jacket, and straightaway look ready to go out, explain that we are compelled to go out, and after a brief round of goodbyes actually do so, leaving behind a greater or lesser amount of irritation depending on the noise we make closing the front door behind us, when we find ourselves down on the street, with limbs that respond to the unexpected freedom they have come into with a particular suppleness, when by this one decision we feel all the decisiveness in us mobilized, when we recognize with uncommon clarity that we have more energy than we need to accomplish and to withstand the most abrupt changes, and when in this mood we walk down the longest streets – then for that duration of that evening we have escaped our family once and for all, so it drifts into vaporousness, whereas we ourselves, as indisputable and sharp and black as a silhouette, smacking the backs of our thighs, come into our true nature.

And all this may even be accentuated if, at this late hour, we go to seek some friend, to see how he is doing.

From *The Sudden Walk*, 1913
(trans. Michael Hoffman, 2007)

Duncan Minshull

– Afterword –

I hope these footsteps across the page, dear walker-reader, taken from familiar and not-so-familiar sources, give you something to think about before the next outing. Of course, shorter utterances, even one-liners, also hit home. The best of these should be inscribed on coffee cups, writ large on T-shirts, or at least try reciting them as you make your way. But out of earshot. You don't want others thinking – ah, here's another of those rambling types. What follow, then, are some of my favourite walking-wisdoms now passed on to you; though never to be declaimed – just whisper them at the ground that's beneath your feet.

It is good to collect things, but better to go on walks.
– *Anatole France*

If I couldn't walk fast and far, I should just explode and perish. – *Charles Dickens*

Health and salvation can only be found in motion.
– *Søren Aaby Kierkegaard*

I have two doctors, my left leg and my right.
– *George Trevelyan*

Walking is simple and primitive; it brings us into contact with mother earth. – *Leslie Stephen*

Solvitor ambulanto – it is solved by walking.
– *St Augustine*

A walk is always filled with significant phenomena.
– *Robert Walser*

All truly great thoughts are conceived by walking.
– *Frederich Nietzsche*

For paths run through people as surely as they run through places. – *Robert Macfarlane*

A walk is only a step away from a story, and every path tells. – *Patrick Leigh Fermor*

Walk fast in the country and stroll about in towns.
– *Frank Tatchell*

Walking is the best way to explore and exploit the city. – *Iain Sinclair*

What peculiarities one finds in big cities when one knows how to roam. – *Charles Baudelaire*

Are you following me? – *Louis Ferdinand Céline*

I choose to walk at all risks. – *Elizabeth Barrett Browning*

Live with intention. Walk to the edge.
– *Mary Ann Radmacher*

She walks in beauty, like the night. – *Lord Byron*

A woman with three cars in her garage will walk for miles, purely for fitness. – *Margaret Visser*

You don't have to do anything to teach your child to walk. – *Dr Benjamin Spock*

Very few men know how to take a walk.
– *Samuel Johnson*

Keep a regular stride, rising on the balls of the feet.
– *Frank Tatchell*

The condition of one's toenails is a key to contentment. – *Nicholas Luard*

I like to have a pocket of raisins to munch at times.
– *Frank Tatchell*

Footwear is tricky. – *John Hillaby*

Silently we unlatch the door . . .
– *Henry David Thoreau*

'*Sehnsucht*' – the passion for what is ever beyond.
– *Robert Louis Stevenson*

Let's go. Route march, burden, desert, boredom,
anger! – *Arthur Rimbaud*

The stream invites us to follow. – *A. H. Hudson*

It was raining hard next morning, too wet for
walking. – *Paul Theroux*

You pass a lot of rubbish as you walk. – *Werner Herzog*

Why is walking so full of woe? – *Werner Herzog*

Once on the road it was all downhill.
– *Samuel Beckett*

Come walk with me – come, walk with me.
– *Emily Brontë*

Walk close to me. I'll shelter you. – *William Barnes*

He walked ahead, and she planted her footsteps in
his. – *Bruce Chatwin*

From Scotland we are marching,
From shipyard, mill and mine.
– *Wal Hannington*

I remembered that a man can outwalk a horse.
– *John Hillaby*

What was the medical name for exceptionally fast walking? Festination! – *John Hillaby*

He was in his old clothes, striding with the tough easy stride of a thousand miles of walking – walking all through his life. – *Christina Stead*

When we die, the wind blows away our footprints.
– *Kalahari Bushmen*

and . . .

There will be many footpaths in Utopia.
– *H. G. Wells*

– Acknowledgements –

Putting together this collection hasn't been a lone effort, one has roamed with others. My thanks go to Kim Kremer at Notting Hill Editions for commissioning the book, to Emma Dickens and Melissa Chevin for their help as well. To Ben Hollands for his illustrations. To Rachel Calder and Sarah Spankie. To Oliver Cookson. And over the years I've enjoyed discussions (and strolls) with various writers who appear here: Lucy Hughes-Hallett, Christopher Hope, Nicholas Shakespeare, Kamila Shamsie and Will Self. Yes, the joys of walking and talking forever . . .

CLASSIC COLLECTION

The Classic Collection brings together the finest essayists of the past, introduced by contemporary writers.

The Russian Soul
– Selections from A Writer's Diary by Fyodor Dostoevsky
Introduced by Rosamund Bartlett

Drawn from Life – Selected Essays of Michel de Montaigne
Introduced by Tim Parks

Grumbling at Large – Selected Essays of J. B. Priestley
Introduced by Valerie Grove

Beautiful and Impossible Things
– Selected Essays of Oscar Wilde
Introduced by Gyles Brandreth

Words of Fire – Selected Essays of Ahad Ha'am
Introduced by Brian Klug

Essays on the Self – Selected Essays of Virginia Woolf
Introduced by Joanna Kavenna

All That is Worth Remembering
– Selected Essays of William Hazlitt
Introduced by Duncan Wu

*All NHE titles are available in the UK, and some titles are available in the rest of the world. For more information, please visit www.nottinghilleditions.com.

A selection of our titles is distributed in the US and Canada by New York Review Books. For more information on available titles, please visit www.nyrb.com.